NEW YORK ABSTAINS "COURTEOUSLY"

Essays on Civil Discourse and Civic Responsibility

Edited by
Marie A. Conn
and
Thérèse McGuire

University Press of America,® Inc.
Lanham · Boulder · New York · Toronto · Plymouth, UK

Dedications

This collection is dedicated in a special way to
Thérèse McGuire, SSJ, PhD
Artist, Scholar, Author, Jewelry and Scenery Designer,
Colleague, Friend

In Honor Of
Bob, Kelsey and Anders, with love and thanks
Ruth O'Neill, SSJ

.

In Memory Of
Alice and Ira Conn
Regis Duffy, OFM

CONTENTS

FOREWORD

The current collection represents the fourth in a series of books of essays by faculty members at Chestnut Hill College. The essays are written by professors who study and teach a wide variety of disciplines. As you might expect from academic scholars, they approach the theme of this latest book, "Civil Discourse and Civic Responsibility," from a wide spectrum of expertise and experience and therefore bring to this important topic, a welcome diversity of perspectives.

The first book in this series, published in 2003, entitled *Balancing the Scales*, presented five essays by five Chestnut Hill faculty members. It focused on how various attitudes, beliefs, and myths presented by generations of male scholars perpetuated an inaccurate assessment of the importance and contributions of women to religion, art, psychology and literature.

The second collection in this series, entitled *Not Etched in Stone*, was published in 2007. It included seven essays from seven Chestnut Hill faculty. These essays focused on the theme of Ritual Memory, Soul and Society, approaching the topic from a historical perspective, a literary perspective and a social science perspective.

The third collection in the series, published in 2010, expanded the number of essays to ten and included faculty from such diverse disciplines as Religious Studies/Holistic Spirituality, Art, English/Communications, Mathematics, Psychology, Education and Human Services. The theme of this collection was differences and diversity presented as a view, a belief, or an opinion that varies from and frequently is diametrically opposed to the "mainstream." As such, the individual or group of individuals who think, act, live, speak, have beliefs which lie outside the prevailing "norm" are considered "the other." As one might expect, over the centuries, such diversity of action, opinion, belief or philosophy has not always been welcomed or accepted.

The themes of this latest collection of essays focus on what it means to be a responsible citizen of our own community and country as well as the global community and world. This collection divides itself naturally into three parts.

In the first part, Marie Conn (Religious Studies), Mary Helen Kashuba (French and Russian), and Barbara Lonnquist (English) review historical examples of both exemplary civil discourse and the dire consequences of the lack of civic responsibility. The first essay of this section examines the wise women of the 15th to 17th century who were the healers of their villages yet were branded as "witches." The next essay compares the French *philosophes*, Montesquieu, Voltaire, and Rousseau, with their American counterparts, Thomas Jefferson, John Adams, and Benjamin Franklin. The final essay of this section discusses John Henry Newman's *Idea of a University* in the light of postmodern theories of knowledge as they interrogate the idea of liberal studies as an enclave exempt from utility.

The second section of the book includes essays by Karen Getzen (English), and Carol Pate (Education) who describe some contemporary applications in their fields. The first essay of this section examines moral action through contemporary illness narratives, with particular attention to the graphic novels *Epileptic* and *Stitches*. This is followed by a discussion on incivility in schools as presented through the lens of the Beyond Intractability Knowledge Base Project of the University of Colorado.

In the final section of this collection Carolynne Ervin (Holistic Spirituality), Nancy Porter (Psychology) and Steven Guerriero (Human Services) shed light on the pitfalls of fundamentalism and offer some avenues to real and fruitful dialogue. This section of essays begins with a review of the dimensions of deep communication/conversation with each other and the effort required to deepen one's listening and responding in ways that foster authentic engagement with another. The second essay in this final section explores the possibility that a lack of flexibility in discourse may partly have its origins in temperamental traits, apparent from the early days of life and thus with biological foundations. The final essay draws from research into the lived experiences of Roman Catholic ecumenists. It offers a developmental model of praxis that may help us better understand the challenges we face in constructing dialogue, creating shared meaning and taking responsible action.

The essays presented in this latest collection provide a wonderful representation of the incredible wealth of knowledge, experience and diverse scholarship of the faculty of Chestnut Hill College. Our students are fortunate to have the opportunity to learn every day from this experience, expertise and scholarship. As a result of this collection, you, the reader, can do the same.

KENNETH J. SOPRANO, PH.D.
Vice President for Academic Affairs
Dean of the Faculty
Chestnut Hill College
Philadelphia, Pennsylvania

INTRODUCTION

Two years ago, just as our third collection of essays, *Imaging the Other: Essays on Diversity* was published, our friend, colleague, and co-contributing editor, Thérèse McGuire, SSJ, faced an unexpected medical challenge. Her first question to me when I visited her for the first time was, "What's our next theme?" Several months later, having endured all the political slings and arrows of yet another election campaign cycle, we had our theme: civil discourse.

McGuire, an art historian, immediately decided that her essay would focus on Thomas More and Henry VIII, and would include the earlier Thomas and Henry, Thomas Beckett and Henry II. Although it finally became clear that she would not be able to complete the essay, she nevertheless has been a big part of this volume. She and I shared hours of conversation about what drew her to More as soon as she considered civil discourse. The short answer is More's total commitment both to his God and to the law. A devoted husband and father, and a boon companion to Henry, More nevertheless chose death rather than deny his conscience. And, no matter how heated debates got, no matter how rigorously he was questioned and challenged, More always responded in a manner that was at once clear and civil. Like Beckett before him, this Thomas had to risk his friendship with his king and even his own life to remain true to what he saw as the right choice. In doing so, Thomas More has left for all of us an example of true civil discourse.

Marie Conn, a theologian, looks at what she describes as an "early smear campaign." According to Conn, from the 15th to the 17th century in western Europe, wise women, the healers of their villages, were branded as "witches," imprisoned, tortured, and condemned to death. Anyone with knowledge of herbs could be targeted; midwives were accused of easing the biblically mandated pain of childbirth. The facile way in which the label "witch" has been used in the recent political campaigns cries out for a new look at this strange phenomenon.

In her essay, Mary Helen Kashuba, SSJ, discusses the Enlightenment ideal of *vertu*. In the 18th century, the good citizen was one who exemplified what the French *philosophes* called *vertu*. *Vertu* included respect and civility toward all members of the community, and also indicated the importance of civic responsibility, patriotism, and devotion to one's country. This essay explores the social and political doctrines of the French *philosophes*, like Montesquieu, Voltaire, and Rousseau, and their American counterparts, men like Thomas Jefferson, John Adams, and Benjamin Franklin.

Barbara Lonnquist looks at civil discourse in the world of the Liberal Arts. As Lonnquist observes, in the political landscape of the last two decades, an increasingly divisive sense of partisanship accompanied by ever-proliferating sources for the rapid, continuous, and often unregulated expression of opinion have posed a considerable threat to the practice and perhaps even the notion of a "civil discourse" in American life. At the same time, the modern university in its partnership with corporate business dismisses the humanities as out of touch. Yet the critical thinking that forms the core of a liberal education is vital to the survival of our democracy.

Lonnquist's essay looks at this debate in the context of mid-century, Victorian England, and more specifically in context of John Henry Newman's *Idea of a University*, which responded to the imperative for a more "utilitarian" education. Central to Newman's argument, and to this essay, is the notion of education as *conversation*. This essay will re-read Newman in the light of postmodern theories of knowledge as they interrogate the idea of liberal studies as an enclave exempt from utility.

Karen Getzen's essay looks at the "Illness Narrative" as a lens through which to look at moral and civil discourse. Although *illness narratives* date to biblical times, there has been a recent proliferation of illness memoirs such that their study is now considered a specialty field or "domain" in their own right. A subgenre of the memoir—the nonfiction illness narrative (often referred to as *pathographies*)—has found favor among a wide readership and covers a range of illness categories from mental illnesses to addiction, disability, and acute and chronic physical illness. Unlike past illness narratives, which most often dealt with illnesses that rather quickly led to death, today's illness narratives also encompass the remission narrative because we live in what one expert has termed a "remission society."

Regardless of the actual form, illness narratives act on multiple specific levels. They "give voice to an experience that medicine cannot describe," as they serve as "stories of self re-invention" and thereby reclaim a body and mind stigmatized as abnormal. Yet beyond the self as a project for change, the illness narrative is "never just a *self*-story but becomes a self/*other*-story." It is this self/other of the illness narrative that is of interest here. The self/other aspect of the illness narrative serves as a form of testimony and a forum to explore the cultural construction of illness (leprosy for example). As such, illness narratives serve not only the self, but also function as a form of moral action. Although the term *moral action* can be ambiguous, it is used here to mean narratives of the body and mind that influence or intervene in social arrangements. The overarching question that is addressed is how the discourse of illness narratives serves the common good. The essay investigates moral action through contemporary graphic illness narratives, with particular attention to the graphic novels *Epileptic* and *The Spiral Cage.*

Education professor Carol Pate takes on the challenge of transformative civility in schools. The goal of her essay is to offer a preliminary polysemous understanding on incivility in schools through the lens of the Beyond Intractability Knowledge Base Project of the University of Colorado, co-directed and edited by Guy and Heidi Burgess. These authors have complied extensive information to assist society to come to an appreciation and understanding of the multiple components of social conflict. After examining the work of Burgess and Burgess, the essay concludes with some thoughts on what might be called transformative civility. The essay is a start, a first conversation, that the author hopes will grow through future dialogue.

Carolynne Ervin's essay on conversation and spiritual direction grows out of her years of experience both as a spiritual director and as someone who trains future practitioners. Ervin has come to believe that, while conversation is a part of everyday life, there are times when it proves to be challenging actually to "hear" what another is saying. Deeper moments of conversation are possible when there is openness to an experience of the Sacred. This kind of conversation is the "stuff" of Spiritual Direction. Her essay illustrates the dimensions of this type of communication with another and points to the effort required to deepen one's listening and responding in ways that foster authentic engagement with another.

Although spiritual direction ordinarily takes place in a one-to-one situation, over the last several years, the professional group *Spiritual Directors International* has encouraged more conversation and understanding among different faith traditions. This is necessary in today's world where diversity involves not only culture and ethnicity but also religious traditions and beliefs. It is vital that we develop ways of communicating which assist us in appreciating the beauty of each individual's uniqueness. This public discourse has only just begun.

Psychologist Nancy Porter takes on the world of fundamentalist thinking in her essay. Questions of spiritual belief and religion and those of human politics are famously the quicksand of civil discourse—the areas in which emotions and a sense of surety underpin opinions which rely on faith, belief, and personality needs and which repeatedly fuel impassioned debate. Porter's essay strives to address findings that support the notion that a fundamentalist approach to the questions of the day are inhibiting to civil debate and fair consideration of all relevant options. The causes and the effects of this situation, felt throughout history and experienced today, will be presented and considered.

Civil discourse is characterized by an ability to listen to ideas beyond, different from, or conflicting with one's own. This essay explores the possibility that a lack of flexibility in discourse may have its origins partly in temperamental traits, apparent from the early days of life and thus with biological foundations.

Finally, Steven Guerriero shares lessons from what he describes as the "ecumenical lifeworld" in an essay that forms an appropriate conclusion to the collection. Fostering the ability to dialogue across diverse issues of faith is arguably one of the most challenging tasks we face. Ecumenists might be viewed as the quintessential boundary-spanners in systems thinking, bridging the divergence among often competing and hostile traditions. There is a great deal we can learn from individuals who have successfully navigated the waters of difference to find constructive and meaningful cooperation and convergence.

Today we are experiencing the depth of ecumenical winter. As we watch the shadows progressively shroud the light of Vatican II, we can ask if there are any valuable lessons we can learn from the experience of ecumenists. Can understanding their lifeworld provide insight into how we can better address the individual and collective lack of civility and respect in our discourse and actions that is played out in our complex and fractious world?

Guerriero's essay draws from research into the lived experiences of Roman Catholic ecumenists. It offers a developmental model of praxis that may help us better understand the challenges we face in constructing dialogue, creating shared meaning and taking responsible action.

Thanks are due to our colleagues for their enthusiasm, our students for providing sounding boards for some of our ideas, and to our Academic Vice-President, Kenneth Soprano, PhD, for his enthusiastic support of this project and his willingness, in the midst of a challenging calendar, to write a Foreword. We owe a particular debt of gratitude to Barbara Crawford, who willingly accepted the onerous task of preparing the camera ready version of our manuscript in the midst of her other responsibilities. Ruth O'Neill, SSJ, MA, Director of the Foreign Language Resource Center, generously agreed to assist us again with the work of copyreading the final draft. We are grateful also to University Press of America for accepting our proposal and bringing our project to fruition.

MARIE A. CONN

CHAPTER ONE

The Victims of the European Witchcraze: An Early Political Smear Campaign[*]

Marie A. Conn

PROLOGUE

During the 2010 mid-term election campaigns, one of the candidates found it necessary to declare that she was "not a witch." It had apparently been learned that this woman had dabbled in some form of Wicca during her high school years. I found the firestorm that followed the revelation and the casual dismissal of it by the candidate personally offensive. From the 15th through the 17th century in western Europe, thousands of women were arrested, imprisoned, tried, convicted, tortured, and executed on charges of "witchcraft." The recent nonsense served to make a mockery of these tragic women and their ordeals.

Political "branding" is nothing new. For more than three centuries in western Europe, wise women, the healers of their villages, were branded as "witches," imprisoned, tortured, and condemned to death. Anyone with knowledge of herbs could be targeted; midwives were accused of easing the biblically mandated pain of childbirth.

---

[*]An earlier version of this essay appeared as "Victims of the Witch Craze: Scapegoats in a Time of Turmoil," a chapter of my book, *Noble Daughters: Unheralded Women in Western Christianity, 13th to 18th Centuries* (Westport, CT: Greenwood Press, 2000), 57–74. Reproduced with permission of ABC-CLIO, LLC.

This essay will explore the strange phenomenon of the European witch hunts. Most of these women died in obscurity. We need to learn their stories, honor their legacy, lift them from the ashes, and give them a voice.

Under the pretext of heresy and then witchcraft, anyone could be disposed of who questioned authority or the Christian view of the world. Witch-hunting secured the conversion of Europe to orthodox Christianity. Through the terror of the witch-hunts, reformational Christians convinced common people to believe that a singular male God reigned from above, that he was separate from earth, that magic was evil, that there was a powerful devil, and that women were most likely to be his agents.[1]

We cannot allow the unfortunate rhetoric of a contemporary election campaign to obscure the lives and the tragic deaths of these women. To speak of "witchcraft" in such a flippant manner brings back the horrors of what has come to be called "the burning time," and makes light of an enormously sad episode in this history of western Europe and western Christianity.

INTRODUCTION

Each year, thousands of visitors pour into Trier in the picturesque Moselle Valley in southwestern Germany. Considered the oldest city in Germany, Trier was founded as Augusta Treverorum in 15 BCE, and, as Roma Secunda, served as a provincial capital of the western Roman Empire in the third century of the Christian era. Tourists delight in the ancient Roman gate, the baths, the museums, and the Hauptmarkt, the main square with its 1,000-year-old market cross.

What most of these visitors don't realize is that, just 300 years ago, other groups flocked to this square, and hundreds like it in small towns and cities throughout western Europe, not to see the sights but to watch women burn. Under the patronage of Johann von Schöneburg, who began his reign in Trier in 1581, "the campaign of Trier was of an importance quite unique in the history of witchcraft. In twenty-two villages 368 witches were burnt between 1587 and 1593, and two villages, in 1585, were left with only one female inhabitant apiece."[2] The cross in the square at Trier is a reminder, for those who know the story, that the Christianization of Europe cost lives.[3]

HISTORICAL BACKGROUND

The fourteenth century in western Europe had been marked by political and cultural dislocations. Terrible economic and social crises resulted from wars and famines, and there was a long series of plagues, most famously the Black Death of 1347–1349.[4] A growing population was suddenly reduced while economic and social institutions like feudalism were being restructured. Farms, villages, and manors were deserted and the growing power of the emerging merchant and industrial classes was leading to a new sense of alienation and a loss of faith in the church that appeared powerless to protect the masses from all these upheavals.[5] The times called for a scapegoat; one answer was the increasing hostility toward women that ultimately expressed itself in the period of the witch-hunts.

In medieval theology the feminine symbolized the physical, lustful, material, appetitive part of human nature, while the masculine symbolized the spiritual, rational, and mental part. This combined with the negative view of marriage and sexuality characteristic of the period, resulted in the justified oppression of women and provided the basis for "the witch-hunting theology that labeled elderly women as fleshly and irrational, even diabolical."[6]

The Canon Episcopi of 906 declared a belief in witchcraft heretical. The canon, which remained in effect from the tenth through the thirteenth century, directed bishops to strive to uproot all kinds of sorcery and magic since these were the means the devil used to deceive people into thinking witchcraft was real and thus abandoning the true God of Christianity. In other words, witchcraft itself was a delusion but one that was capable of undermining the church.[7]

By the twelfth century, however, frightening images of devils and witches on broomsticks began to appear. The church was now portraying witches in terms usually applied to heretics: "a small clandestine society engaged in antihuman practices, including infanticide, incest, cannibalism, bestiality and orgiastic sex."[8] Scholasticism, the medieval theology developed in the universities, was one force that changed the attitude toward witches. According to the Scholastics, the deeds of the witches were absolutely real. In his Summa Theologica, Thomas Aquinas makes this quite clear and it is, according to Julio Baroja, the work of Aquinas that "goes far to explain the increased violence of persecution and the categorical return to the doctrine laid down in Exodus 22:18: 'Thou shalt not suffer a witch to live.'"[9]

Stuart Clark notes that "in the sixteenth and seventeenth centuries a predisposition to see things in terms of binary opposition was a distinctive aspect of the prevailing mentality." In this period marked by a "preoccupation with the extreme poles of the religious and moral universe," witchcraft beliefs represented the orthodox world reversed or inverted to such an extent that every facet of demonism was read as an actual or symbolic inversion of traditional life.[10] Indeed, sanctity and witchcraft were sometimes regarded as mirror images of each other.[11]

> While the relationship between the holy and unholy could be studied in virtually any historical context, it was in late medieval Europe that it became a particularly important issue, partly because society was increasingly complex: rising lay literacy gave wider access to spiritual literature and spiritual exercises, and the proliferation of religious orders, societies, and movements brought with it an unwieldy assortment of folk whose multiform pious activities were met with equally manifold distrust. Perhaps never before in the history of Christianity . . . were there so many people distrustful of each other's pieties. What could be more natural in such a culture than suspicions, first whispered and then shouted aloud, that the pretense of sanctity was a mask for the worst form of impiety?[12]

Where prior to the fifteenth century people had distinguished between "white witchcraft," or healing, and "black witchcraft," or evil, in the sixteenth and seventeenth centuries a third category emerged, "evolved by churchmen and lawyers from Christian theology, canon law and certain philosophical ideas. . . . The witch became a witch by virtue of a personal arrangement with the Devil who appeared to his potential recruit in some physical form."[13]

> As the Inquisition was developed to rid the true church of heretics, so now its powers were extended to deal with the even greater danger of women in league with the devil. Witches were perceived to be the mirror image of true mystics: as true mystics experienced God, so these women experienced communion with the devil. . . . The engagement of ecclesiastical authority with who should count as a mystic, and its gendered nature, could hardly be clearer.[14]

"The papacy and the Inquisition had successfully transformed the witch from a phenomenon whose existence the Church had previously rigorously denied into a phenomenon that was deemed very real, very frightening, the antithesis of Christianity, and absolutely deserving of persecution."[15]

THE INQUISITION

"While moral justice was impossible, given the presupposition of the Church that it had the right, even the duty, to persecute those who differed in their religious beliefs, legal justice in sixteenth century terms was indeed dispensed by the Roman Inquisition."[16]

By the early Middle Ages heresy had been "clearly defined as organized groups of people propagating ideas that represented more than simple opposition to the Church, and which threatened the basis of medieval society."[17] The church was becoming increasingly centralized and powerful, a reality that "reached its zenith during the pontificate of Innocent III (1198–1216), the first and most important of the great lawyer-popes who dominated the thirteenth century."[18] "Heresy is an invention of the Middle Ages. From about the eleventh century, churchmen increasingly worried about heresy, and in 1179 the Third Lateran Council issued a strong decree against the various forms which it believed it could discern. From that point forward, the inquisitors were kept busy hunting heretics and seeking to purge the church of them."[19]

Prior to Pope Innocent III there had already been a gradual shift from a reluctant tolerance of heresy to persecution of the offenders. In 1184 the first sign of an official policy appeared in the form of a bull (a papal document that affects matters of importance), *Ad abolendam*, issued by Pope Lucius III. The bull ordered bishops to "make inquisition" for heresy, but local bishops proved ineffective. It was left to Innocent to conceive of a coordinated policy.

When Innocent called the Lateran Council in 1215 he had two main objectives: the Holy Land crusades and the suppression of heresy. Canon 3 specified harsh measures against heretics and warned "lax" bishops that they would be removed from their posts. The Inquisition itself dates to the early pontificate of Pope Gregory IX, becoming a reality sometime between 1227 and 1233. In 1231 the constitution *Excommunicamus* contained detailed legislation for the punishment of heretics. Gregory entrusted this work to the Mendicant Orders founded by Dominic and Francis. "The enthusiasm with which some of them took to this new task, represents one of the most curious episodes in the history of the church."[20]

Pope Innocent IV, in the bull *Ad Extirpanda*, declared civil power subservient to the Inquisition, insisting that the uprooting of heresy was the chief duty of the state and introducing torture into inquisitorial procedure. The bull also condoned burning at the stake for relapsed heretics. In 1298 the system of repression instituted by Innocent II and honed by popes Alexander IV, Urban IV, and Clement IV, was codified by Pope Boniface VIII in his *Liber Sixtus*.[21] Eventually, all these measures were accorded theological respectability in Aquinas' *Summa*. Although Aquinas did not deal specifically with witchcraft, he expressly condemned both implicit and explicit pacts with the devil. "[Aquinas' work] was the crucial link that allowed the Inquisition to shift its attention from outright heretics to magicians and sorcerers, and inquisitors often cited Aquinas between 1323 and 1327 when attacking the invocation of spirits as heresy."[22] The *Summa* also approved of punishment as a spiritual good. The Inquisition thus gained both theoretical and moral justification.

The Inquisition took witchcraft seriously, which led the people to believe in its reality. Edward Burman observes that the combination of inquisitorial efficiency and the adoption by the secular courts of inquisitorial techniques embedded the reality of witchcraft in the European consciousness.[23] "The church created the elaborate concept of devil worship and then used the persecution of it to wipe out dissent, subordinate the individual to authoritarian control, and openly denigrate women."[24] "The separate Dominican streams of violent physical repression and theological argument merged in the inquisitorial persecution of witchcraft. . . . The power and guile of the essentially Dominican antiwitch Inquisition helped to fix in the popular imagination an irrational concept that might otherwise have played a minor role in European history."[25]

By the end of the fourteenth century municipal courts had adopted inquisitorial techniques. Informers were no longer required to substantiate their accusations in these courts. Formerly, judicial procedure operated under the "talion"—a statute that demanded that any accuser who failed to convince a judge of the validity of his or her case suffer the same penalty that the accused would have suffered if found guilty.[26] Once the talion was abolished, accusations were facilitated, and the task of the inquisitors was more and more not to discover the truth but to elicit confessions. In fact, in 1578 inquisitor Francisco Peña declared that the main purpose of a witch's trial and execution was not the salvation of the accused's soul but the advancement of the public good. This was done by putting fear into the hearts of the onlookers.[27]

Christine Larner sees the era of the witch-hunts as a period of transition from restorative, interpersonal justice to abstract, rational, bureaucratic justice with repressive sanctions, marked by a "shift in responsibility from the accuser to the court official, which had the effect of making frivolous or vindictive accusation possible. . . . [This] system of abstract justice . . . made possible the victimless crime of simply being a witch, of being the servant of the Devil."[28]

There is also evidence that inquisitors became rich through the witch-hunts, which involved bribery and the confiscation of the accused's money and property. Some witches were even condemned posthumously, their bodies dug up and burned, and their heirs' property confiscated. The families of the accused were responsible for all expenses connected with the imprisonment, including food and clothing, and even whatever costs were connected with the execution.[29] "Victims were charged for the very ropes that bound them and the wood that burned them. Each procedure of torture carried its fee. After the execution of a wealthy witch, officials usually treated themselves to a banquet at the expense of the victim's estate."[30] In 1592 Father Cornelius Loos, who had accompanied many victims to the stake, observed: "Wretched creatures are compelled by the severity of the torture to confess things they have never done . . . and so by the cruel butchery innocent lives are taken; and by a new alchemy, gold and silver are coined from human blood."[31] "The essential characteristics of what is commonly called witchcraft—a combination of maleficium, night-flights, sabbat, and pact with the Devil—were assembled in the period that ran from 1320–1486, and the Inquisition was responsible at least in part for this assemblage and for the great increase in witch trials at the end of the fifteenth century."[32] In a period when any challenge to the church was seen as a challenge to society, the judges of both the secular courts and the inquisition believed they were acting as God's agents but many got carried away with ecclesiastical self-righteousness. Those accused of witchcraft were seen as rebels against church and state just at a time when the two were completely identified.[33]

THE VICTIMS

Even a skeptic like Robin Briggs, who takes great pains to point out that many of the victims of the witch craze were indeed men, goes on to observe: "It remains true that most accused witches were women."[34]

> It becomes increasingly clear that the realities of popular life and belief do not accord at all with the official concept of witchcraft. The victims of the witch-hunts were not witches in the sense of the official demonologists' definition, although once subjected to torture many victims may have come to believe in the witch-hunter's definition of themselves as night-flying witches in pact with Satan.[35]

The traditional teaching of Christianity was that women were oversexed, rationally and morally inferior to men, and spiritually deficient. "The church, having sown the wind in its teaching about women, was now reaping the whirlwind." Sanctity was attributed to men, witchcraft to women.[36] Late medieval sermons, as well as popular stories and songs, denounced women's "slippery and manipulative" nature, betraying the misogynist tradition that lay at their roots.[37] Herbert Richardson notes that the period of witch persecutions coincided with the period of courtly love. "The Witch . . . was nothing other than the counterface of the Lady. She was the one who objectified all those anxieties and negative feelings that late medieval man would not allow to enter into his imagination and feelings about his Lady."[38] The witch was the one onto whom medieval man projected his fears of women.

By the 1500s the models of the female saint and the witch were virtually mirror images of each other. Each was possessed, the one by God, the other by Satan; each could read minds; each was capable of "flying," the one through levitation, the other through the air; each bore wounds, the one the stigmata, the other the so-called devil's mark. Each was, in her own way, a threat to ecclesiastical authority.[39]

Grace Jantzen also points to the developing capitalist economy which put men and women in competition with each other.[40] On the other hand, women who were poor, old, single, or widowed were seen as a drain on the resources of those involved in the developing economy. So, persecuting these women as witches acted as an important, gender-specific, method of social control.[41]

> The witch in many cases was the poorest of the poor, dependent on her neighbors to stave off starvation. In the sixteenth century, . . . the poor were becoming poorer; more peasants were forced to beg or steal in order to survive. Old, single women, especially vulnerable to this economic crunch, came to be seen as nuisances. When they turned them down, people felt guilty, an uncomfortable state exacerbated when the beggar cursed them for their refusal. Then when misfortune occurred, people turned on the beggars, a classic example of "blaming the victim."[42]

The most common victim was the old woman who resembled the Crone. "Common people of pre-reformational Europe relied upon wise women and men for the treatment of illness rather than upon churchmen, monks or physicians."[43] Wise women combined knowledge of medicinal herbs and pleas for divine assistance; thus, they offered medicine that was both more affordable and more effective than that offered by church-licensed physicians. "Denied the ancient role of clergy or the newly emerging one of doctor, women drew on their own networks of information and skills inherited from their mothers to serve as privileged counselors and practitioners."[44] Orthodox Christians, however, were taught that such healing was evil since health was to be left in God's hands and so the role of the healer became suspect.

The church branded anyone with knowledge of herbs as a witch. "Mere possession of herbal oils or ointments became grounds for accusation of witchcraft."[45] Midwives were also targeted. Childbirth was considered defiling, but the real "sin" of the midwives was easing the pains of childbirth, pains that had been divinely ordained as a result of Eve's "original sin."[46] No less an authority than Martin Luther had observed: "If [women] become tired or even die, that does not matter. Let them die in childbirth—that is why they are there."[47] As Helen Ellerbe notes, "It is hardly surprising that women who not only possessed medicinal knowledge but who used that knowledge to comfort and care for other women would become prime suspects of witchcraft."[48] Partly as a result of the witch-hunts, medicine became an exclusively male preserve and the Western tradition of herbal medicine was virtually destroyed.

The period of the witch trials marks the first time that women were criminalized on such a large scale. Usually, women's behavior had been considered the responsibility of the father or husband. Since, in patriarchal societies, men determined who was a "good woman," anyone deviating from their standards was vulnerable to charges of witchcraft as were any who exhibited "male" characteristics, like independence or aggression, or those who failed to fulfill female roles by remaining unmarried or, when married, by not bearing children. "The stereotype witch is an independent adult woman who does not conform to the male idea of proper female behavior. She is assertive; she does not require or give love (though she may enchant); she does not nurture men or children, nor care for the weak. She has the power of words—to defend herself or to curse."[49] So, the same patriarchal misogyny that gave men leave to beat their wives ultimately sanctioned the torture and execution of thousands of "witches."

> As for the status of women in European legal history, one notable fact about them is their absence. Until the sixteenth century, women made up a very small number of the defendants, accusers, or witnesses in legal cases. . . . Then around 1560 European secular courts began to hear accusations of witchcraft and sexual crimes, and women began to appear in court in large numbers, an entirely new phenomenon . . . in the process of bringing these offenses under their jurisdiction, sixteenth-century courts were forced to admit their perpetrators to a new legal standing. . . . That European women first emerged into full legal adulthood as witches, that they were first accorded legal status in order to be prosecuted for witchcraft, indicates both their vulnerability and the level of antifeminism in modern European society.[50]

Unlike the Anabaptist martyrs, whose letters and theological tracts fill the pages of Martyrs' Mirror,[51] the victims of the witch-hunts died leaving behind virtually no written records. One letter, however, does survive, written in 1590 by Rebecca Lemp to her husband. "Oh, husband, they take me from thee by force. How can God suffer it? My heart is nearly broken. Alas, alas! My poor dear children orphaned. Husband, send me something that I might die or I must expire under torture. If thou canst not do it today, do it tomorrow. Write to me directly. R. L."[52]

The torture which Rebecca Lemp feared so much was indeed horrifying. After being stripped, shaved, and searched with needles for the "mark of the devil," which could be any wart or birthmark, the accused witch was tortured in order to obtain the necessary confession. In addition to the mask of shame, the dressmaker's collar, and the ducking stool, women accused of witchcraft faced unbearable pain inflicted by thumb and leg screws, the iron maiden, and head clamps. Gresillons crushed the tips of fingers or toes in a vise; the échelle, or rack, violently stretched the body; while the strappado jerked the body in mid-air. The witch-chair was a seat of spikes which could be heated from below. Should a woman be strong enough to withstand the first round of torture, a second, more intense, session followed. The few who still held out were subjected to the "third degree" of torture which usually ended in death.[53]

Women convicted of witchcraft were usually burned to death. In 1197, Pedro II of Aragon had decreed that relapsed heretics should be burned; in 1198, Innocent III extended this mandate to include heretics who were not affected by excommunication. Once witchcraft was looked upon as heresy, this tradition of burning heretics turned against the accused witches. Why fire? Perhaps by burning the witches, those in power hoped to reduce the sorcery these women were accused of to ashes. Jeffrey Russell suggests that the choice of fire "is explained on the deepest levels by the purificatory power attributed to that element in most mythologies, and in Christianity the choice was reinforced by the analogy with hell and by the numerous examples of purificatory fire in the Old and New Testaments.[54]

> That this torture was carried out in the presence of large crowds often numbering in the thousands gave it a ritual meaning beyond that of simple punishment. As a public purging of evil, it declared that the land was rid of demonic enemies and that not a trace of their hated presence remained. Once the condemned had been reduced to ashes, those very ashes would be thrown in the wind or scattered over moving water. But public witch executions were more even than a purging: they affirmed that the ruler who ordered them was godly, and even more important, that his power was greater than the forces of evil.[55]

In other words, the public burning of witches served to assure the people both that the power of the devil had, at least for the moment, been overcome, and that church and state were in safe, strong hands. The execution also sent a strong message to other women not to consort with midwives or healers, and even to fear and distrust all others of their sex.

THE *MALLEUS MALEFICARUM*

"By the end of the fifteenth century, a whole doctrine of witchcraft had been developed together with a technique of systematic persecution."[56] Two Dominican inquisitors, Heinrich Institor Kraemer and Jakob Sprenger, successfully sought a bull from Pope Innocent VIII authorizing them to root out witchcraft. Two years later, in 1486, they compiled the *Malleus Maleficarum*[57] (Hammer against the Witches), a handbook to guide those involved in the apprehension and conviction of witches. The bull from Innocent was printed before the text itself, thus adding papal weight to the volume. "What is most striking about the *Malleus* is its preoccupation with sexual functions and its vicious attack on women in general."[58]

> The author's purpose was clear. Witchcraft was a vast and vile conspiracy against the Faith; it was on the increase; witches were depopulating the whole of Christendom; and, through the impotence of the secular courts, these creatures remained unpunished. The *Malleus* was written to demonstrate precisely what witches were doing, and how they could be stopped. It first establishes the truth of the existence of witchcraft and its heretical nature; then elucidates the principal evils practised by witches and demons; and finally lays down formal rules for initiating legal action against witches, securing their conviction, and passing sentences upon them.[59]

The arguments in the Malleus rested on three underlying beliefs. Witchcraft was real and it would be heresy to deny it. Demons constantly interfered with human life. And both witchcraft and demonic activity were allowed by God for God's own purposes. Furthermore, although Satan could work alone, he preferred to work through witches, offering greater offense to God usurping God's own creatures.[60] "When it was published, [the *Malleus*] carried on its title page the bold epigraph, *Haeresis est maxima opera maleficarum non credere,* 'to disbelieve in witchcraft is the greatest of heresies.' It was the exact opposite of the ruling of the Church in the Dark Ages. Since the 9th century, the wheel had come full circle."[61]

> The authors of the *Malleus* used many weighty sources, mainly Aristotle, who provides both natural explanation and the logical structure of each proposition; the Scriptures, which form the basis for all theological, miraculous, and moral arguments; St. Augustine, whose assertions concerning magic and demonology are scattered broadcast throughout the text; and St. Thomas Aquinas, who furnishes a synthesis of the other three major sources.[62]

The *Malleus* used the scholastic method of the *Summa*, stating a question, then giving arguments, and finally reaching conclusions. The manual, by shifting the blame for sorcery onto women with exaggerated and misogynistic force, "created the popular view of the witch as a woman that survives today; in that respect it was truly a seminal work."[63] Women, after all, having been formed from a bent rib, were deficient and more given to carnal lust, and easily provoked.[64] Although filled with circular arguments and essentially flawed, the book was extremely influential.

The *Malleus* took the position that women were especially susceptible to witchcraft because they are feebleminded, weak in faith, and cursed with an almost insatiable sexual desire which led them to lust for the devil. Men were urged to express their gratitude to God for sparing them the degradation of being born female.

Witches were thought to have special powers over the sexual and reproductive functions. Moreover, they were also believed to have a dampening effect upon male potency, though the authors of the *Malleus* hedge on the point of whether witches actually had the power to undermine male sexual capacity (to the point of removing their genital organs) or whether such problems were the result of a bewitching delusion of "glamour," as they called it. The authors gave a theological rationale for their overwhelming stress on venereal functions: God permitted witches "more power over this act, by which the first sin was disseminated," than over other human actions.[65]

Other parts of the *Malleus* detailed the correct procedures to be followed in witchcraft trials, including the various forms of tortures which could be used to extract confessions. "The judicial process advocated in the *Malleus* is inexorable; its inquisitorial procedures were, theoretically, implacable; and technically there would appear to have been no escape once a witchcraft accusation had been initiated."[66] Barbara Roberts has observed that the scientific revolution relied on the techniques of the Inquisition in the witch interrogations. Francis Bacon advised "teasing" or "torturing" the secrets out of Mother Earth.[67] Dominican Matthew Fox, who subtitles the *Malleus*, "How to Burn a Witch," characterizes the handbook as a "pure study of repression and projection," reflecting men's fears of sexuality, of the dark, and of women.[68] "The *Malleus Maleficarum* is an unsurpassed revelation of the primal anxiety about women that lurks in the heart of every man."[69] "It would not be far-fetched to describe the book as a cross between a scholastic work and a pornographic magazine."[70]

The production of manuals like the *Malleus* undoubtedly increased the likelihood of trials. Larner has pointed out that Mainz and Bamberg, two cities where the most numerous trials occurred, were early centers of printing.[71]

CONCLUSION

The witch craze has been described as "the shocking nightmare, the foulest crime and deepest shame of western civilization."[72] And yet, left alone, peasant societies would never have engendered such a phenomenon. "For centuries the wise women and other healers who worked on the frontiers of magic had existed side by side with the Church even in moments of tension."[73] It was the institution of the inquisitorial procedure and the extensive trials in both ecclesiastical and secular courts that transformed the beliefs of the people concerning witches into a "highly effective means of social control."[74]

Why did the witch craze last so long? Russell speculates:

The most fundamental reason for the longevity of witchcraft may be that, after the terrors of the fourteenth century made the image of the witch more vivid than ever before, the political power of the prince and the popes, the procedures of the Inquisition, the harsh strictures of canon and civil law, and the opinions of the theologians united to fix that vivid picture in the European mind almost indelibly.[75]

The peak of the witch craze came as Europe was in a period of transition, a time Burman has described as the "maximum moment of wrenching between a medieval world-view and that of a recognizably modern Europe, between the years 1570 and 1630."[76]

Just as there seems to be no one cause for the eruption of the witch craze, so there is no one reason for its decline. Factors most commonly cited include the weakening power of both Catholic and Protestant clergy; the rise of nationalism; and the development of the scientific method. Jantzen adds another factor, namely, a seventeenth-century change in gender ideology "which would affect the social control of women without any need to have recourse to witch persecutions."[77] Prior to the period of the witch trials, women had been viewed as largely passive. But accusations of witchcraft required active women, "capable of entering into a devious and passionate relationship with the devil, and able to be a threat to people around her, and, in the eyes of the inquisitors, so great a danger to the church that no method of torture and extermination was too extreme."[78]

In the pre-industrial economy, however, it suited men's purposes better to reassert women's passivity. If women were once again viewed as weak and incapable of reasoning or moral decision making, they could more easily be restricted to the home and the needs of the children. This meant, however, that they could not at the same time be cunning, active witches, so the persecutions ended, at least in part, due to "the new gender construction resting on the infantilisation of women."[79]

Even the emerging scientific method was expressed in gendered terms. Bacon observed that philosophy, which was masculine, had the task of penetrating the secrets of nature, understood as feminine. Where the masculine was active, virile, and generative, the feminine was passive, weak, and waiting.

> To say that it was the rise of science by itself which discredited belief in witches is too simple. The combination of new economic patterns, new religious structures, and the new "masculine" science all worked together to develop a new variety of the social control of women, based on her passivity and inferiority. It can hardly be insignificant that the witch hunts ceased just when they were no longer necessary as a means of asserting male dominance.[80]

The role of the church must also be acknowledged. Much of what was done was done "with the permission of God," a phrase used whenever other arguments proved inconsistent or implausible. "It is an argument favoured by Catholic theologians and Reformers alike; and it reveals a colossal arrogance on the part of those who believe that their vapid subtleties really do elucidate the most intimate divine purposes which they alone fully comprehend. It is impossible to argue rationally against those who have been taken entirely into God's confidence."[81]

It took more than 200 years of terror and death but the church finally transformed the image of paganism into devil worship and folk culture into heresy. The ancient celebrations of the earth goddess eventually became civil carnivals presided over by men. "No monuments have been built to their memory. Only a few relics, like the witch's cart, remain to mark their passing."[82] Six generations of children watched as their mothers burned at the stake, and the effects of the burning times are still with us. Women still struggle to find their voice, to tell their story, to proclaim their truth.

Scholars debate over the how and the why of the "witch craze," alternately exonerating or condemning the Inquisition, subscribing to or denying the impact of natural disasters like the Black Death, estimating and re-estimating the actual number of executions, until library shelves are filled with volumes and readers are left shaking their heads. Underlying all these opinions, however, is the grim reality that, between the fourteenth and seventeenth centuries women died apparently just for being women. It is a macabre and terrible period in the history of Western Christianity, and one that must not be forgotten.

NOTES

1. Helen Ellerbe, *The Dark Side of Christian History* (San Rafael, CA: Morningstar Books, 1995), 137–138.

2. Hugh R. Trevor-Roper, "Witches and Witchcraft: An Historical Essay (II)," *Encounter* 28 (1967), 16–17.

3. "The Burning Times," Part Two of the Series, *Women and Spirituality*, video produced by The National Film Board of Canada, 1990.

4. Anne Barstow speculates that the Black Death actually prevented an outbreak of witchcraft accusations in the fourteenth century by "almost providentially killing off" Europe's excess population. When conditions worsened in the sixteenth century and no such plague occurred, the people needed some other means for resolving tensions, namely, witchcraft accusations. Anne Llwewellyn Barston, *Witchcraze: A New History of the European Witch Hunts* (San Francisco: Pandora, 1994), 100.

5. Jeffrey Burton Russell, *Witchcraft in the Middle Ages* (Ithaca: Cornell University Press, 1971), 169–170.

6. Caroline Walker Bynum, *Holy Feast and Holy Fast: The Religious Significance of Food to Medieval Women* (Berkeley: University of California Press, 1987), 262.

7. Julio Caro Baroja, "Witchcraft and Catholic Theology," in Bengt Ankarloo and Gustav Henningsen, eds., *Early Modern European Witchcraft: Centres and Peripheries* (Oxford: Clarendon Press, 1993), 26. The *Canon Episcopi* appeared in a work entitled *De ecclesiasticis disciplinis* by Regino, abbot of Prüm in Germany, who died in 915.

8. Margot Adler, *Drawing Down the Moon* (New York: Beacon Press, 1979), 49.

9. Baroja, "Witchcraft," 27–28.

10. Stuard Clark, "Inversion, Misrule and the Meaning of Witchcraft," *Past and Present* 87 (May 1980), 105, 118.

11. Richard Kieckhefer, "The Holy and the Unholy: Sainthood, Witchcraft, and Magic in Late Medieval Europe," *Journal of Medieval and Renaissance Studies* 24 (Fall 1994), 355.

12. Kieckhefer, "Holy and the Unholy," 359.

13. Christina Larner, *Witchcraft and Religion: The Politics of Popular Belief* (Oxford: Basil Blackwell Publisher Ltd., 1984), 3.

14. Grace M. Jantzen, *Power, Gender and Christian Mysticism* (New York: Cambridge University Press, 1995), 269.

15. Ellerbe, *Dark Side*, 121.

16. John Tedeschi, "Inquisitorial Law and the Witch," in Ankarloo and Henningsen, eds., *Early Modern European Witchcraft*, 85.

17. Edward Burman, *The Inquisition: The Hammer of Heresy* (New York: Dorset Press, 1984), 16. Much of the history of the Inquisition in this section is drawn from Burman.

18. Burman, *Inquisition*, 17.

19. Jantzen, *Power, Gender*, 246.

20. Burman, *Inquisition*, 34.

21. Church law had been collected into five books edited by Raymond Peñafort in 1234. Book V, *De Haereticus*, contained the principal constitutions of the Inquisition. Boniface, in the "sixth book," added all the later bulls.

22. Burman, *Inquisition*, 123.

23. Burman, *Inquisition*, 127.

24. Ellerbe, *Dark Side*, 114.

25. Burman, *Inquisition*, 124–125.

26. Jantzen, *Power, Gender*, 268.

27. Ellerbe, *Dark Side*, 76.

28. Larner, *Wtichcraft and Religion*, 59–60.

29. Ellerbe, *Dark Side*, 80.

30. Barbara Walker, *The Woman's Encyclopedia of Myths and Secrets* (San Francisco: Harper & Row, 1981), 1086.

31. Russell Hope Robbins, *The Encyclopedia of Witchcraft and Demonology* (New York: Bonanza Books, 1981), 16.

32. Burman, *Inquisition*, 117.

33. Russell, *Witchcraft*, 3.

34. Robin Briggs, *Witches & Neighbors: The Social and Cultural Context of European Witchcraft* (New York: Penguin Books, 1996), 261.

35. Richard A. Horsley, "Who Were the Witches? The Social Roles of the Accused in the European Witch Trials," *Journal of Interdisciplinary History* 9, no. 4 (Spring 1979), 712.

36. Larner, *Witchcraft and Religion*, 61. See also M. G. Dickson, "Patterns of European Sanctity: The Cult of Saints in the Later Middle Ages" (unpublished doctoral dissertation, University of Edinburgh, 1974).

37. Rosemary Radford Ruether, *Women and Redemption: A Theological History* (Minneapolis: Fortress Press, 1988), 187. See also Mary Potter Engel, "Historical Theology and Violence against Women: Unearthing a Popular Tradition of Just Battery," in Mary Potter Engel and Walter E. Wyman, eds., *Revisioning the Past: Prospects in Historical Theology* (Minneapolis: Fortress Press, 1992), 51–76.

38. Herbert W. Richardson, *Nun, Witch, Playmate: The Americanization of Sex* (New York: Harper & Row, 1971), 64.

39. Bynum, *Holy Feast*, 23,

40. Jantzen, *Power, Gender*, 270–272.

41. Marianne Hester, *Lewd Women & Wicked Witches: A Study of the Dynamics of Male Domination* (London: Routledge, 1992), cited in Jantzen, *Power, Gender*, 274.

42. Barstow, *Witchcraze*, 26.

43. Ellerbe, *Dark Side*, 131.

44. Barstow, *Witchcraze*, 109.

45. Ellerbe, *Dark Side*, 132–143. See also Jeanne Achterberg, *Woman as Healer* (Boston: Shambhala, 1991).

46. Many cultures considered childbirth defiling, due to the blood involved. Consequently, there are many rituals of purification prescribed for women following childbirth, for example, the Catholic custom of the "churching of women," an outgrowth of the Jewish rite of purification, performed forty days after the birth of a boy and eighty days after the birth of a girl.

47. Karen Armstrong, *The Gospel According to Women: Christianity's Creation of the Sex War in the West* (New York: Doubleday, 1987), 69. It was also Luther who wrote that the witch should not be compared to the virgin but to the good wife, since, by being obedient to her husband, a woman would avoid the temptation to use magic. See Ruether, *Women and Redemption*, 127–128.

48. Ellerbe, *Dark Side*, 136.

49. Larner, *Witchcraft and Religion*, 62, 84.

50. Barstow, *Witchcraze*, 41.

51. See my essay, "The Anabaptist Martyrs: The Radical Commitment of 'Others'," in Marie A. Conn and Thérèse McGuire, Eds., *Imaging the Other: Essays on Diversity* (Lanham, MD: University Press of America, 2010), 19–42.

52. "The Burning Times."

53. Hugh R. Trevor-Roper, *The European Witch-Craze of the Sixteenth and Seventeenth Centuries and Other Essays* (New York: Harper Torchbooks, 1967), 120–121. See also "The Burning Times" and "Witches," an installment of the A&E series, *Ancient Mysteries*, 1996.

54. Russell, *Witchcraft*, 150–151.

55. Barstow, *Witchcraze*, 143.

56. Hugh R. Trevor-Roper, "Witches and Witchcraft: An Historical Essay (1)," *Encounter* 28, no. 5 (May, 1967), 8.

57. Heinrich Kraemer and Jakob Sprenger, *Malleus Maleficarum*, Montague Summers, trans. (London: Pushkin Press, 1948).

58. Elizabeth Clark and Herbert Richardson, *Women and Religion: A Feminist Sourcebook of Christian Thought* (San Francisco: Harper San Francisco, 1977), 118.

59. Sydney Anglo, "Evident authority and Authoritative Evidence: The *Malleus Maleficarum*," in Sydney Anglo, ed., *The Damned Art: Essays in the Literature of Witchcraft* (London: Routledge & Kegan Paul, 1977), 15.

60. Anglo, "Evident Authority," 15–16. Anglo goes on to point out that "the whole argument for persecution rests upon a monstrous paradox, since witches are merely serving God's mysterious purposes." If God permits the devil to work through human agents, why aren't the witches praised instead of blamed?

61. Trevor-Roper, "Witches and Witchcraft," 15.

62. Anglo, "Evident Authority," 18.

63. Burman, *Inquisition*, 130.

64. Anglo, "Evident Authority," 16. Anglo notes that the "monkish misogyny of the *Malleus* is blatant."

65. Clark and Richardson, *Women and Religion*, 118. See *Malleus Maleficarum*, part 1, question 6 and part 2, question 1.

66. Anglo, "Evident Authority," 28.

67. Barbara Roberts, in "The Burning Times."

68. Matthew Fox, in "The Burning Times."

69. Clark and Richardson, *Women and Religion*, 120.

70. Jantzen, *Power, Gender*, 266.

71. Larner, *Witchcraft and Religion*, 57.

72. Robbins, *Encyclopedia*, 3.

73. Burman, *Inquisition*, 189.

74. Horsley, "Who Were the Witches," 713–714.

75. Russell, *Witchcraft*, 170.

76. Burman, *Inquisition*, 190. Horsley also notes the difficult transition from one economic-political system to another, a transition that enabled the authorities to induce the peasants to blame their troubles on "witches." By attacking these witches, society was able to unburden itself of troublesome elements. Horsley, "Who Were the Witches," 714.

77. Jantzen, *Power, Gender*, 274.

78. Jantzen, *Power, Gender*, 275.

79. Jantzen, *Power, Gender*, 275.

80. Jantzen, *Power, Gender*, 275–276.

81. Anglo, "Evident Authority," 21.

82. "The Burning Times."

CHAPTER TWO

Vertu: An Enlightenment Ideal

Mary Helen Kashuba, SSJ

In the eighteenth century, the good citizen exemplified what the French *philosophes* called *vertu*. Among other things, it includes respect or civility to all other members of the community. *Vertu* also addresses the importance of civic responsibility, patriotism, and devotion to one's country. It involves social responsibility, and regulates the conduct of an individual in regard to others. The person who possessed *vertu* led a frugal yet productive life, shared with others, and contributed to the general welfare. The luminaries of the American Enlightenment used the word virtue in much the same sense.

This essay explores the social and political doctrines of the French *philosophes*, especially Montesquieu, Voltaire, and Rousseau, with special emphasis on references to *vertu*. Montesquieu delineates three forms of government in his *Esprit des Lois (The Spirit of Laws)*, which greatly influenced the early American legislators. However, one of his most accessible works is the story of the Troglodytes, an imaginary people who exemplify both the spirit and the corruption of democracy as presented in *L'esprit des lois*. Voltaire created a similar story in his famous parable of Eldorado. Rousseau's *Discourse on Inequality* and *Social Contract* address the same theme. All emphasize civility and civic responsibility.

The American *philosophes*, notably Thomas Jefferson, John Adams, and Benjamin Franklin, echo these ideas. Their thought borrowed in great measure the ideals of French and British Enlightenment figures. They use the word "virtue" to describe their vision of the civic-minded individual. The correspondence between

Thomas Jefferson and John Adams frequently alludes to this ideal, while Benjamin Franklin's wit throughout his *Autobiography* and *Poor Richard's Almanac* addresses the same points.

In addition, both French and American artists of the eighteenth century portray people and situations embodying the ideal of *vertu*. Among the French painters one might note Jacques-Louis David, whose pre-revolutionary paintings, such as *The Oath of the Horatii*, exemplify the ideal of the citizen whose sense of civic responsibility overpowers personal relationships. The famous American artist Benjamin West portrayed an idealized society in *Penn's Treaty with the Indians*. Other artists likewise exalted civic responsibility in the new Republic.

La Déclaration des droits de l'homme et du citoyen[1] and the American *Bill of Rights* summarize Enlightenment thought and address the concept of *vertu*. The French *Déclaration*, written in 1789 as a prelude to the Revolution, exerted tremendous influence throughout those fateful years as well as in future generations. However it often deviated from its original purpose. Furet explains, "The *Declaration of the Rights of Man* is explained not so much by what it borrowed—from Locke as well as Montesquieu, from Rousseau as well as the American state constitutions—as the need to which it responded: to redefine the sphere of politics in liberty and law."[2]

While the *Déclaration* does not prescribe any specific duties, it speaks of the responsibilities of all people as members of society:

> The representatives of the French people, constituted as a National Assembly, considering that ignorance, forgetfulness, or scorn of the rights of man are the single causes of public misfortune and the corruption of governments, have resolved to expose, in a solemn Declaration, the natural, inalienable, and sacred rights of man, so that this Declaration, constantly present to all the members of the social body, may recall to them unceasingly their rights and duties.[3]

The Virginia *Declaration of Rights*, the predecessor and inspiration for the French *Déclaration* and the American *Bill of Rights*, states more explicitly: "That no free government, or the blessings of liberty, can be preserved to any people but by a firm adherence to justice, moderation, temperance, frugality, and virtue and by frequent recurrence to fundamental principles."[4] It clearly shows the influence of Enlightenment thought.

Montesquieu's *Histoire des Troglodytes*, found in Letters 11–14 of *Les Lettres Persanes*,[5] contains a concrete example of these ideas. He believed that a story would prove more valuable than a philosophical digression. Uzbek, an imaginary Persian visiting Paris, attempts to respond to his friend Mirza's questions; namely, does happiness consist in the pleasures of the senses or in virtue, and are virtue and justice innate or acquired. This important concept leads Montesquieu and other authors to examine the relevance and utility of religion.

Uzbek's story recounts an imaginary Arabian people, called Troglodytes. The first Troglodytes lived in the state of nature and led evil lives. A foreign king could not rule them; therefore, they killed him and his family. They then elected magistrates, but the same fate befell these officials. Not only did they lack consideration for their rulers, but they also failed to show civility to one another, living only for their individual gratifications. Finally a plague afflicted them. Fortunately a generous doctor healed them. They refused to pay him, and when the plague recurred, he allowed them to perish. Thus their race was exterminated except for two virtuous families.

These two families worked hard for the common good, had strong family values, and were blessed with many children. They held festivals for the gods "where joy reigned no less than frugality." Their religion consisted in thanksgiving, which helped to reinforce their natural virtue. They held all things in common, and spent as much time as possible in service to one another. They educated their children in virtue, often recalling the evil that befell their ancestors.

The virtue practiced by the good Troglodytes contained all the marks of civility and civic responsibility. Montesquieu illustrates this in Letter XIII, noting their mutual assistance, collaboration in the fields, and respect for parents. Against their will, they were obliged to enter into a defensive war against their enemies who wrongfully attacked them. The Troglodytes sacrificed their lives willingly for the sake of the nation, and overcame their enemies. Even then, they treated the conquered peoples with civility and respect.

Because of their growth in numbers, they decided one day to choose a king. This was their undoing. They elected an elder, recognized for his virtue and knowledge. Like Samuel in the Bible who warned the Hebrews of the dangers of a king, the elder chided them: "Your virtue is beginning to weigh heavily on you. In your present state, not having any leader, you must be virtuous in spite of yourselves: otherwise you could not subsist. . . . I will soon see my sacred ancestors once again. Do you expect me to tell them that I have left you under any yoke other than that of virtue?"[6]

Anecdotes from travelers who had visited primitive peoples and observed their behavior inspired Montesquieu and other eighteenth-century writers. As a consequence, most *philosophes* believed that human nature was naturally good and inclined to virtue. Crisafulli argues that the first part of Montesquieu's allegory refutes Hobbes, since it demonstrates that the state of nature does not result in government. In fact, an evil state of nature leads to destruction.[7] On the contrary, the second society appears to be naturally virtuous, although Montesquieu is ambiguous in this regard. He seems to conclude that human nature tends toward the good and rejects evil. People realize that in promoting the common good, they also promote their own. Therefore they will practice virtue instinctively, given the proper circumstances, and especially the appropriate government. Crisafulli demonstrates Shaftesbury's influence on Montesquieu in formulating this thesis:

> Montesquieu and Shaftesbury conceive virtue as resulting essentially from the moral-social instincts attributed to man by the Stoics. For both of them, virtue or

goodness in man consists in his acting according to his natural inclinations toward public good, and can only exist in relation to his fellowmen in society. It is in this sense that Montesquieu's good Troglodytes are naturally virtuous.[8]

Montesquieu's distinction between virtue and nature, and between virtue and religion reappears in the writings of Rousseau and Voltaire, among others.[9] In the mind of many Enlightenment writers, although religion supported *vertu*, it did not cause its existence, since they saw *vertu* as a natural phenomenon. In fact, any religion could support *vertu*. Thus, it is from "utility and morality that (Montesquieu's) advocacy of religious toleration stems; for intolerance destroys in part at least the utility of religion, while if religion is essentially ethical, divergences of dogma and cult become matters of indifference."[10] Like most moralists of his time, Montesquieu separated religion from virtue, but advocated it for the social benefits it brought.

Montesquieu returns to the question of virtue in *L'Esprit des Lois*. He notes that *vertu is the principle of a democratic government*.[11] Without vertu ambition enters in, and with it avarice and corruption. *Vertu* necessitates frugality, for luxury brings with it the desire for the wealth of others. It fosters selfishness, where one does not make the common good the highest priority. Like the land of the Troglodytes, the republic without *vertu* will perish.[12] Montesquieu often points to the Romans, a people he studied in great detail. Their life of luxury and self-indulgence led to their demise, since self-interest destroyed the primacy of the common good.

Montesquieu had reservations about the success of a democratic republic, indicating that monarchy probably presented the most efficient form of government, if it did not degenerate into tyranny or despotism. He admits that *vertu* can thrive in a monarchy, but with a different motivation, which he calls honor (*honneur*). In a fragmentary sequel to the original *Lettres Persanes*, published among his *Pensées*,[13] Montesquieu follows the Troglodytes after they have chosen a king. The first king died, and his successor, also a wise and just man, feared that with the introduction of commerce and the arts people would prefer wealth to virtue. A wise Troglodyte reminded him that only if the people refused avarice and prodigality would virtue continue to exist. The king should base rewards, not on wealth, but on justice. The King responded, "Je vous déclare, que, si vous n'êtes pas vertueux, vous serez un des peuples les plus malheureux de la terre. Dans l'état où vous êtes, je n'ai besoin que d'être plus juste que vous."[14] (I declare to you, that if you are not virtuous, you will be one of the most miserable people on earth. In the state where you are, I need only to be more just than you.) Thus, the king must practice a higher degree of virtue than the citizens. He concluded, "O Troglodytes! Nous pouvons être unis par un beau lien: si vous êtes vertueux, je le serai; si je suis vertueux; vous le serez." (O Troglodytes! We can be united by a beautiful bond: if you are virtuous, I will be also, and if I am virtuous, you also will be.)

Unlike many of his contemporaries, Montesquieu did not insist on an agrarian society to promote virtue. In discussing the parable of the Troglodytes, Keohane observes, "He (Montesquieu) believes that the crucial factor here is a set of attitudes on the part of the citizens and not how they make their living."[15] She goes on to state the values prized by Montesquieu. Education for civic virtue heads the list. Citizens must also prefer the common good to individual interests. Devotion to the republic must supersede all other passions. This requires self-renunciation and comes at a cost. While a virtuous republic may be difficult to attain, it is not impossible.

Voltaire develops a similar story of *vertu* in his famous parable of Eldorado in *Candide*. Candide, a naïve young man, believes that "all is for the best in the best of all possible worlds," based on the philosophy of Leibnitz, which Voltaire seeks to refute. Candide travels throughout the world in search of his beloved, Cunégonde, and in the course of his voyage learns much about life in general. When he reaches Eldorado, he finds a country where the children play with precious gems and homes resemble palaces. Puzzled, Candide and his companion Cacambo enter a restaurant where the hosts receive them with great civility and invite them to partake of an elegant meal at no cost.[16]

Wishing to learn more about this Paradise, they speak with an elder of the country, who explains the system to them. The citizens of Eldorado have only one religion, which consists in thanking God. No priests are necessary, since every father fulfills the role of priest in his family. Law courts do not exist, nor do jails, nor is there unemployment, since all have honorable work. Candide's visit culminates in an interview with the King, who bears more resemblance to the head of a democracy than to a monarch. One does not bow to him, but rather embraces him. The two visitors dine lavishly with the King, and speak to him as one would to any ordinary citizen.

Interestingly enough, Candide does not wish to stay in Eldorado. He alleges the absence of Cunégonde as his reason. Although no one normally left this hidden Paradise, the King tells the travelers that freedom is the hallmark of the country. The citizens will keep no one there without his or her consent. Candide and Cacambo depart, taking with them gold and gems which were without value in Eldorado, but most desirable in the rest of the world. Unfortunately, they quickly lose the treasures. In fact, they encounter many other adventures which might make them wonder why they left Eldorado!

Voltaire leaves us with a dilemma: is this ideal life impossible? Or is it possible only within a small, highly-structured society, safe from outside interference? Like Montesquieu's Troglodytes, the citizens of Eldorado could maintain their life style only by a strong sense of civic responsibility and right relations with one another. While they lived comfortably, they did not amass wealth but shared it willingly with one another. They aimed for progress, and worked on scientific pursuits to improve society. They exercised generosity and hospitality, and like the good Troglodytes, practiced a religion of thanksgiving without any trappings of conventional piety. Thus they grew and developed in their natural virtuous state. In fact, Bottiglia maintains that deism was the mortar that held the small state together, perhaps an indication that religion does affect virtue![17] On the other hand, he also states that Candide had to leave Eldorado because he was not yet philosophically ready for it, and later realizes that it was at least approachable, if not attainable.[18]

Voltaire is more of a moralist than a philosopher, since he produced no systematic method. He insisted far more on a virtuous life than on the means to get there. Henry notes: He (Voltaire) writes in his *Philosophe ignorant*, "soit que la matière puisse penser ou non, quiconque pense doit être juste" (whether matter thinks or not, whoever thinks must be just) and in *Les Lettres philosophiques*: "il importe peu à la Religion de quelle substance soit l'âme, pourvu qu'elle soit vertueuse."[19] (It matters little to religion of what the substance the soul is composed, provided that it be virtuous.) Voltaire admired the Quakers, not for their religious expressions, which somewhat repulsed him, but rather for their acceptance of all people as their brothers, their hatred of war, and their religious tolerance. In fact, he seems to indicate that they came closer than any other group to exemplifying the ideal society of Eldorado.[20]

Jean-Jacques Rousseau, another great French *philosophe* who reflected on *vertu* and nature, apparently never agreed with Voltaire. In fact, their relationship consisted in constant conflict. However, they often reached similar conclusions. Rousseau also sought for an ideal society. Disillusioned by social inequality which he blamed on private property, he too imagined a world where *vertu* would reign as it did when people lived simply without the trappings of luxury and jealousy. He described them in his *Discourse on Inequality* and *Social Contract*. Primitive people, he maintains, did not suffer from our modern vices: excessive leisure or excessive work, self-indulgence among the rich, or unhealthy nutrition among the poor, and unbridled passions.[21] Virtuous persons, on the other hand, "lived by the work of their hands, and nourished their souls with the most sublime truths."[22]

For Rousseau, the formation of civil society led to problems. People became jealous, coveted one another's property, and abandoned simplicity of life. However, Rousseau did not wish to return to the primitive world, although he deplored the theory of progress so dear to most other *philosophes*. He found in it the danger of excessive luxury, to the detriment of frugality, which for him and for Montesquieu formed one of the fundamental bases of *vertu*. While Montesquieu's Troglodytes regretfully chose a king, Rousseau proposed the idea of the *volonté générale*, or "general will," which led the citizens to abandon some part of their freedom to insure the well-being of the whole. They would then choose a Sovereign, who would bring out their best interests. Montesquieu believed that people should be virtuous for the sake of virtue, and reluctantly allowed a ruler, although he later admitted a virtuous one. Rousseau also saw the inherent difficulties in this ideal and admitted the necessity of a strong leader, one however empowered by the people.

Rousseau allowed any religion that would support the sociability necessary for the smooth functioning of the state. "There is therefore a purely civil profession of faith whose dogmas the sovereign must determine, not specifically as dogmas of religion, but as sentiments of sociability, without which it is impossible to be a good citizen or a faithful subject."[23] An essential part of sociability is equality, which no sovereign power can abolish. Rousseau insists on the responsibility of each person towards the members of the community. He prescribes that the group dismiss anyone who practices intolerance. For him, *vertu* consists in working together for the common good. Indeed, religion at the service of the state was a widespread conviction in the eighteenth century, despite Enlightenment ideals of freedom and tolerance. Even during the French Revolution, which outlawed Catholicism, the leaders established the "cult of the Supreme Being," as a way unifying the nation and promoting *vertu*.

While pessimistic by nature, Rousseau held an optimistic view of human nature. He maintained that pity or compassion for others formed the basis of *vertu*, since human beings experience repugnance at the sight of others' suffering. This should naturally lead all people to do good to others, and to consider their well-being.[24] His famous Vicaire Savoyard, or the Pastor of Savoie, echoes this idea in *Emile*, where conscience emerges as the source of virtue, always choosing what is best.[25]

Eighteenth-century French thinkers prioritized the diffusion of scientific and political knowledge. The *philosophes*, under the leadership of Denis Diderot and Jean D'Alembert, participated in an ambitious project which evolved into the *Encyclopédie*, originally aimed at translating the English *Cyclopedia* by Chambers. It quickly became a forum for the expression of radical ideas. The Church condemned it and publicly burned copies. Needless to say, it quickly developed an underground market and became a best-seller.

Not all the *Encyclopédie* articles contained radical ideas, however. Many of them simply encourage the practice of *vertu*. The authors of the *Encyclopédie* warn against excessive luxury. In the article *Luxe*, the author, Saint-Lambert, denies that the excessive wealth of a few brings down a nation, but rather maintains that inefficient and immoral government will ruin it. If those who govern show indifference to the public welfare, he writes, "that is reason enough for the disappearance of all strong patriotic feelings."[26] One can easily see the indictment of the unjust social system of France and rural impoverishment, imputed to the failures of the monarchy. Rousseau noted the same failure in his Discourse on Inequality. In order to subordinate luxury and reestablish the equilibrium of wealth, Saint-Lambert prescribes bringing relief to the countryside as the first step. This means a reduction of privileges, and work by all. Like Montesquieu, Saint-Lambert insists on a well-regulated society where everyone contributes to the common good.

Thomas Jefferson, well-schooled in the writings of Montesquieu from his childhood, echoed a number of these sentiments in his First Inaugural Address. Among the qualities essential for citizens of a republic, he lists "entertaining a due sense of our equal right to the use of our own faculties, to the acquisitions of our industry. . .honesty, truth, temperance, gratitude, and the love of man. . .a wise and frugal government, which shall restrain men from injuring one another, which shall leave them otherwise free to regulate their own pursuits of industry and improvement."[27] Jefferson believed in the simple life in the country, noting that those who labor in the earth are the chosen people of God, and that rarely does one see corruption of morals among them. In this he echoes Rousseau, who deplored the city and its temptations, and insisted that the virtuous person work close to nature.

Thomas Jefferson notes that before the establishment of the American states, only the old world system of government with all its vices existed. Now, he maintains, a new order is imperative, adapted to a situation in which everyone, "by his property, or by his satisfactory situation, is interested in the support of law and order."[28] He distinguishes between natural and artificial aristocracy. The latter, based on wealth and birth, without either virtue or talent, is unacceptable. The former, with virtue and talent, is a great gift of nature, to be used for the instruction and government of society. He notes the revolution of thought taking place in Europe, one "of science, talents, and courage, against rank and birth, which have fallen into contempt."[29]

John Adams, a great friend and correspondent of Thomas Jefferson, likewise emphasized the ideal of the virtuous person. As early as 1776, Adams opts for a republic, maintaining that although it "may beggar me and my children," it will produce "strength, hardiness, activity, courage, fortitude, and enterprise."[30] He might become rich in a monarchy, but it would encourage frivolity and luxury. He continues, "Under a well-regulated commonwealth, the people must be wise, virtuous, and cannot be otherwise. . . . Virtue and simplicity of manners are indispensably necessary in a republic among all orders and degrees of men." Ever practical, however, he recognizes that virtue is not a common trait among people. Even in America, he sees the enemies of virtue, servility and flattery. How could one bring the new nation to virtue? Not unlike Rousseau, he feels that a great leader can do this, and hopes that one such person will emerge in the new republic. This also recalls Montesquieu, who believes in the leader's virtue as crucial in promoting the same ideal in the subjects.

In a letter to Benjamin Rush in 1811, Adams reiterates his belief "that religion and virtue are the only foundations, not only of republicanism and of all free government, but of social felicity under all governments and in all the combinations human society."[31] However, he hastens to add that he does not wish to make a statement on religion, lest he be accused of favoring one religion above another. Like Montesquieu, Voltaire, and Rousseau, he accepted religion as a means of promoting civic virtue. He was appalled that France during its Revolution could ever think of establishing a republic of virtue on a base of atheism, and had strong reservations about the outcome of the Revolution, many of which proved true.

The tone of frugality that animates Montesquieu and Thomas Jefferson comes to life in the aphorisms of Benjamin Franklin, the author of the famous *Poor Richard's Almanac*:

A penny saved is a penny earned.

The poor man must walk to get meat for his stomach, the rich man to get a stomach to his meat.

If you know how to spend less than you get, you have the Philosophers-Stone.

He that buys by the penny, maintains not only himself, but other people.

The excellence of hogs is fatness, of men virtue.

He that lives well, is learned enough.

All things are easy to Industry, All things difficult to Sloth.

Don't value a man for the Quality he is of, but for the Qualities he possesses.

An innocent Plowman is more worthy than a vicious Prince.

He (the rich man) does not possess Wealth, it possesses him.

A Penny sav'd is Twopence clear, A Pin a day is a Groat a Year. Save & have. Every little makes a mickle.[32]

And many others like these, some original, others imported from various authors whom Franklin had read in his lifelong friendship with books, among them Montaigne,[33] insure the immortality of this *Almanack* which appeared from 1732–1757, and which sold up to 10,000 copies a year.

In his *Autobiography*, Benjamin Franklin describes a plan he had developed to attain moral perfection. He listed thirteen virtues with their precepts. Among them one finds frugality: "Make no expense but to do good to others or yourself; i.e., waste nothing." Industry: "Lose no time; be always employed in something useful; cut off all unnecessary actions." Sincerity: "Use no hurtful deceit; think innocently and justly; and, if you speak, speak accordingly." He began his list with temperance, maintaining that this is the chief of all virtues. He devised a little score sheet to mark his successes and failures.[34] It is certainly a system to be admired!

The writings of the *philosophes* stress the importance of education in maintaining virtue. The good Troglodytes kept the lessons of the past alive by recounting the story of the wicked ancestors to their children. When these lessons began to fade, however, virtue ebbed away. Benjamin Franklin wrote in 1750: "Nothing is of more importance for the public weal than to form and train up youth in wisdom and virtue."[35] While the American *philosophes* were all well-educated men, Benjamin Franklin was self-educated. At age twelve he began to work for his brother as a printer. However, he later founded the American Philosophical Society, the Academy that developed into the University of Pennsylvania, and composed scientific and cultural treatises. Thomas Jefferson asked to be remembered for three accomplishments: he was the author of the Declaration of Independence, of the Statute of Virginia for Religious Freedom, and Father of the University of Virginia. These remain inscribed on his tombstone, and emphasize his commitment to education and to virtue.

The French *philosophes* also were learned men. Montesquieu had received a strong background in law. Voltaire received a classical education with the Jesuits, as did Diderot, who originally prepared for the clerical state. Rousseau, like Benjamin Franklin, was basically self-educated. At a time when free education did not exist, they nevertheless sought to bring learning to others, especially through the *Encyclopedia*. Victims of censorship themselves, the *philosophes* fought fearlessly for freedom of the press and freedom of expression. They had popularized this notion based on the ideals of English writers.[36] Following their lead, the authors of the *Déclaration des droits de l'homme et du citoyen* declared, "The free communication of ideas and opinions is one of the most precious rights of Man: every citizen may thus speak, write, and print freely, except to abuse this freedom, in cases determined by the law."[37]

Although many critics characterize the eighteenth century as frivolous and licentious, the concept of *vertu* often appears in popular festivals. One of these was the Rose Festival, which originated in Salency, a hamlet near Noyon in Picardy. The rural people had the custom of choosing a chaste young woman whom they crowned as *rosier*, or "queen of virtue." The young woman received a dowry of twenty-five livres. The villagers led her in procession and honored her publicly. The festival spread throughout northern France, and at least a dozen plays embody this theme. Eventually not only young women received this honor, but virtuous older folk as well.

The celebration of virtue lasted throughout the Revolution, and well into the nineteenth century. Sarah Maza explains: "If under the pens of its promoters the rose festival attained the status of a myth, it was a singularly rich and malleable myth, which could conjure up visions of rural arcadia, notions of power and community, and allegorical representations of civic virtue revolving around a female figure."[38] The symbol of the chaste virgin, well-known in antiquity, came to signify the simplicity of country life, the absence of slavery and poverty, responsible landowning, and rural peace. Maza continues, "Under the pens of lawyers, the Picard village became a republic of small proprietors deftly handling the plow, a country located somewhere between Montesquieu's allegorical nation of Troglodytes and the social ideals of the sans-culottes' utopian vision, in sum, of what the realm of France could become under the rule of young Louis XVI."[39] It also became a political image, where "the queen of virtue created for a day the egalitarian, unmediated 'transparency' of hearts that was Rousseau's political dream."[40] One might note that Rousseau, who condemned the theater, approved this type of entertainment as an expression of republican virtue.

Not only do we find rural celebrations in honor of virtue, but in the late eighteenth century the French Academy, the Academy of Bordeaux, and the Academy of Montauban organized annual virtue prizes (*prix de vertu*). These prizes allowed social elites to designate particular acts as "virtuous."[41] Normally urban middle classes received this award, a "duty-based" prize. The French Academy, and the others as well, stipulated that "the author of the celebrated action, man or woman, cannot issue from a social position above that of the bourgeoisie, and it is desirable that this person be chosen from the lowest ranks of society." One of the many examples describes the rescue of three young children from the frozen waters at Versailles. Another praises a faithful servant of Jean-Baptiste Réveillon. On the eve of the French Revolution, she rescued her master's business documents from the rebels who burned and looted the establishment.

The *Prix de vertu* honored "first, those who performed isolated acts of extraordinary heroism and second, those who displayed an exceptional level of dedication to a social superior (such as the domestic servants who garnered the vast majority of awards)."[42] The award aimed at encouraging emulation, in the hopes that the lower classes, thus rewarded for doing their duty, would inspire the upper classes in the same vein. These prizes multiplied considerably throughout the late eighteenth century and into the days of the French Revolution, which did its best to promote a "republic of virtue."

Finally, let us examine the ways in which the visual arts reinforced this concept of vertu. French paintings of the last half of the eighteenth century consisted primarily of two types: the Rococo and sometimes frivolous works of artists such as Boucher and Fragonard, and the more realistic designs of painters such as Chardin and Greuze. Diderot, an art-critic as well as a *philosophe*, writes of Boucher's work, "What colors! What variety! What richness of objects and ideas! This man has everything, except truth."[43] He describes Fragonard's *Tableau ovale représentant des groupes d'enfants dans le ciel* thus, "Mr. Fragonard, this is terribly dull."[44] In addition to criticizing the style, he lamented the absence of *vertu*.

On the other hand, Diderot bestows high praise on Jean-Baptiste Greuze (1725–1805). He admires *Le fils puni*,[45] exhibited in sketch-form in the Salon of 1765. This is a companion piece to the *Malédiction paternelle (The Father's Curse)*, in which the father directs his anger against his son. The sole support of his family, he had left for an adventure in the army, and answered his father's reproaches with insults. In *Le fils puni (The Son's Punishment)* the son returns home, injured and maimed, at the moment of his father's death, too late to make amends for his conduct. After praising the artistic aspects of Greuze's painting, and describing the subject, Diderot emphasizes the moral virtues it inspires: "What a lesson for fathers and children!"[46] He notes the depth of pity evoked by these paintings in contrast to the popular yet frivolous style of Boucher's works, "Boucher aura plus tôt vendu cinquante de ses indécentes et plates marionnettes que Greuze ses deux sublimes tableaux."[47] (Boucher could have sold fifty of his indecent and flat puppets faster than Greuze [could sell] these two sublime paintings.)

Jean-Baptiste-Siméon Chardin (1699–1779) excelled in still life scenes and bourgeois interiors. Referring to Chardin's work for the Salon of 1759, Diderot remarks, "It is always nature and truth."[48] The *Benedicite* ranks among the paintings that Diderot admires for its color, composition, and originality, as well as for its subject taken from ordinary bourgeois life. It portrays a young mother and her daughter saying grace before a simple meal. Chardin stands out as a pioneer in depicting such scenes, not previously considered worthy of art. He also offers a valuable documentary of life in the eighteenth century. Diderot likewise admired *Woman returning from the market* for its technique and its artistic merits, as well as for the vision of reality and devotion to duty that it inspired.

Finally, the work of Jacques-Louis David (1748–1825) fostered the ideal of *vertu* and patriotism, before, during, and after the Revolution. Perhaps the most famous painting is *The Oath of the Horatii* (1784), inspired by Corneille's sentiment of duty, *devoir*, and Enlightenment values. The three sons must ignore their wives and families and embrace the republican ideal symbolized by their father who raises their swords aloft. They must face either death for themselves or for the members of their family as they engage in a single-handed combat with the enemy. The painting also serves as a model of neo-classical art which found expression in other works by David, such as *The Death of Socrates*. His depiction of *The Death of Marat* became a revolutionary icon, portraying Marat as more of a Christian martyr and a Christ figure than a leader of the Terror. Later on, David went on to portray Napoleon in scenes larger than life, thus pursuing the ideal of patriotism in a new regime.

American art, finding its inspiration in the European world, insisted perhaps even more strongly on virtue and patriotic values. Many American artists studied in London and Paris, and flourished in and around Boston and Philadelphia. One of the best-known, Benjamin West, was born of Quaker parents in 1738 in Springfield (now Swarthmore, Delaware County), PA, a short distance from Philadelphia. He studied art in Philadelphia and New York City, and later in Italy. Because of the paucity of scholarly artists in America, he went to England in 1763, where he remained until his death in 1820. George III of England appointed him historical painter, and in this capacity he executed a number of works with political overtones, among them *The Burghers of Calais*, a call to protest and freedom.[49]

Benjamin West fostered the eighteenth-century ideal of virtue in *Penn's Treaty with the Indians* (1771–1772), currently at the Pennsylvania Academy of Fine Arts. The painting conveys an image of idyllic family life among the native Americans. At the bottom right a mother lovingly caresses her children. In the center, tribal chiefs engage in peaceful negotiations with William Penn and his delegation. The background denotes an atmosphere of prosperity, with newly-built homes on the shore and numerous boats on the river. The friendly encounter with the Americans recalls the utopian dreams of thinkers such as Montesquieu, Voltaire, and Rousseau. William Penn's son Thomas commissioned this work to emphasize how well Pennsylvania had flourished thanks to his father's wise policies.[50]

Benjamin West influenced other American painters, among them John Singleton Copley, Gilbert Stuart, and Charles Wilson Peale. John Singleton Copley was considered the finest artist in colonial America. He was born in Boston in 1738 and died in London in 1815. His portrait of Paul Revere (1768–1770) shows a pensive patriot holding a silver tea-pot. The son of a French Huguenot, Paul Revere (Rivoire)[51] was also a prosperous and prominent Boston silversmith. For this reason, as well for Paul Revere's patriotism, Copely featured the tea-pot in his portrait.[52] Paul Revere also executed an engraving of the Boston Massacre of 1770, based on an etching by his half-brother, Henry Pelham.[53]

American artists in the late eighteenth and early nineteenth-century excelled in portrait painting. Frequently they chose their subjects from among America's heroes, thus producing patriotic icons for the new Republic. Both Gilbert Stuart (1755–1828) and Charles Wilson Peale (1741–1847) painted numerous portraits of George Washington. Gilbert Stuart's best-known portrait of Washington appears on the one dollar bill. Stuart's other patriotic works include a portrait of Paul Revere in 1813 at the age of seventy-eight. The skillful use of black and white emphasizes Paul Revere as an elder statesman, dignified and composed.

A native of Maryland, Charles Wilson Peale came to Philadelphia in 1776 because of his enthusiasm for the new American republic. He had studied art under Benjamin West, and served in the American Revolution. He portrayed Thomas Jefferson (1791) as an idealist and a thinker, a true *philosophe*. Charles Wilson Peale is the father of artists, Raphaelle, Rembrant, and Titian, and the uncle of still others, who continued his patriotic tradition. In true Enlightenment fashion, he pursued natural history, and established a museum in Baltimore, later known as the Peale Museum (now a historical monument).[54] Thomas Jefferson donated numerous fossils from his own collection. The museum later became the depository of the collection from the American Philosophical Society, founded in 1743 by Benjamin Franklin. Not unlike Voltaire's Eldorado, where scientific pursuits engaged this utopian and virtuous society!

Thomas Jefferson believed in aesthetics as a means of attaining virtue. "Rather than a morality ruled by either reason or science, Jefferson adumbrated . . . an aesthetics of virtue, a fusion of art and morals, whereby reflective beings are capable of discerning the path to virtue through aesthetic experience. For Jefferson, in short, aesthetics charted avenues of direction for virtuous conduct."[55] His plans for Monticello pay tribute to both art and virtue. Quinby continues:

> Monticello represents a fitting icon of his aesthetics of virtue. High atop the leveled plateau of a mountain, Monticello stands serenely overlooking the wilderness landscape that envelops it and provides a striking contrast to its classical architecture. To reach Monticello, visitors must pass through the sublimity of the "workhouse of nature" before entering the tranquillity and harmony of the human-made edifice. And, once there, the ingress through nature remains ever visible as a symbol of what humanity, working in concert with nature, may achieve.[56]

In examining these Enlightenment figures, we can discern the relevance of their message, for their own day and ours. Their works remain among the classics of human thought. They have inspired generations of people in the Western world and even beyond. They proposed to establish a new society in which virtue and equality would reign. In a world where technology, globalization, and instant communication have revolutionized human encounters, modern society would do well to heed the ideals of respect for the common good, education in civic values, and right relations. The Enlightenment thinkers and artists believed that virtue was inherent in human nature, and under the proper circumstances would flourish, in their day, and in days to come. The land of the Troglodytes, Eldorado, and the Republic of Virtue were approachable, if not attainable. In the words of Thomas Jefferson, "it is the manners and spirit of a people which preserve a republic in virtue."[57]

NOTES

1. Pascal Nicollier (Fribourg, 1995), *Déclaration des droits de l'homme et du citoyen, with commentary*. www.liberte.ch/wp-content/uploads/ddhc.pdf.

2. François Furet and Mona Ozouff, *A Critical Dictionary of the French Revolution*. (Cambridge MA: The Belknap Press of Harvard University Press), 1989, 665, 674.

3. "Les Représentants du Peuple Français, constitués en Assemblée nationale, considérant que l'ignorance, l'oubli ou le mépris des droits de l'homme sont les seules causes des malheurs publics et de la corruption des Gouvernements, ont résolu d'exposer, dans une Déclaration solennelle, les droits naturels, inaliénables et sacrés de l'homme, afin que cette Déclaration, constamment présente à tous les membres du corps social, leur rappelle sans cesse leurs droits et leurs devoirs."

4. Bill of Rights: *The Virginia Declaration of Rights*. US National Archives. www.archives.gov/exhibits/charters/virginia_declaration_of_rights.html.

5. Montesquieu, Lettres Persanes. (Paris: Garnier-Flammarion); 1964. Lettres 11 à 14, 37–44.

6. Ibid., 44. "Votre vertu commence à vous peser. Dans l'état où vous êtes, n'ayant pas de chef, il faut que vous soyez vertueux malgré vous: sans cela vous ne sauriez subsister. . . . Je vais bientôt revoir mes aïeux sacrés. Pourquoi voulez-vous . . . que je sois obligé de leur dire que je vous ai laissés sous un autre joug que celui de la vertu?"

7. Allessandro S. Crisafulli, "Montesquieu's Story of the Troglodytes," in *Charles-Louis de Secondat, Baron de Montesquie*, ed. David Carrithers (Surrey, England and Burlington Vt: Ashgate), 2009, 42.

8. Ibid., 48–49.

9. Ronald Grimsely, "The Idea of Nature in the *Lettres Persanes*," *Charles-Louis de Secondat*, ed. David Carrithers, 40.

10. Roger B. Oake, "Montesquieu's Religious Ideas," *Journal of the History of Ideas* (Vol. 14, No. 4 Oct., 1953), 550, www.jstor.org/stable/2707701.

11. Montesquieu, *L'Esprit des Lois*. Livre III, 3. (Paris: Garnier), 1961.

12. Ibid., Livre VIII, 2.

13. Charles-Louis de Secondat, *Pensées et fragments inédits, Tome 1*. (Bordeaux: Gounouilhou), 1899. #120, 51–54. books.google.com/books?id=TNRcAAAAMAAJ& printsec=frontcover&dq=montesquieu+pensees&source=bl&ots=RseuZsNkBb&sig=YTux vLt5y1rkbtLtnPRa-gkgqxo&hl=en&ei=dFF2TduQOa2Q0QGA9sXcBg&sa= X&oi=book_result&ct=result&resnum=2&ved=0CB0Q6AEwATge#v=onepage&q&f=false.

14. Ibid., 53.

15. Nannerl O. Keohane, "Virtuous Republics and Glorious Monarchies," in *Charles-Louis de Secondat, Baron de Montesquieu*, ed. David Carrithers, 222.

16. Voltaire, *Romans et contes. (Paris: Garnier-Flammarion)*, 1966, 214–221.

17. William F. Bottiglia, "The Eldorado Episode in *Candide*," *PMLA*, 1958, 339.

18. Ibid., 343.

19. Patrick Henry, "Voltaire as Moralist," *Journal of the History of Ideas*, Vol. 38, No. 1 (Jan.–Mar., 1977), 145, www.jstor.org/stable/2708846.

20. Graham E. Rodmell, "A Quaker Prisoner in France (1756)," *Eighteenth-Century Studies* (Vol. 7, No. 1 Autumn, 1973), 80, www.jstor.org/stable/3031613.

21. Jean-Jacques Rousseau, *Du contrat social et autres œuvres politiques.* (Paris: Classiques Garnier), 1975, 45.

22. Ibid., 31.

23. "Il y a donc une profession de foi purement civile dont il appartient au souverain de fixer les articles, non pas précisément comme dogmes de religion, mais comme sentiments de sociabilité, sans lesquels il est impossible d'être bon citoyen ni sujet fidèle." Jean-Jacques Rousseau, *Du contrat social.* (Paris: Garner-Flammarion), 1966, 179.

24. Hartley Burr Alexander, "Rousseau and Political Humanitarianism." *The Journal of Philosophy, Psychology and Scientific Methods*, Vol. 14, No. 22 (Oct.25, 1917) 601, www.jstor.org/stable/2940308.

25. Jean-Jacques Rousseau, *Émile.* (Paris: Garnier-Flammarion), 1966, 373.

26. Nellie S. Hoyt and Thomas Cassirer, *Encyclopedia.* (New York: The Bobbs-Merrill Company), 1965, 216.

27. Adrienne Koch, *The American Enlightenment.* (New York: Braziller), 1968, 406.

28. John Adams, *The Adams-Jefferson letters.* (Chapel Hill: The University of North Carolina Press), 1988, 388.

29. Ibid., 391.

30. Koch, 182.

31. Ibid., 212.

32. Benjamin Franklin, *Poor Richard's Almanac.* Coded, edited and translated by Rich Hall for the Independence Hall. www.richhall.com/poor_richard.htm.

33. Robert Newcomb, *Benjamin Franklin and Montaigne. Modern Language Notes*, Vol. 72, No. 7 (Nov., 1957), 489, www.jstor.org/stable/3043511?seq=2.

34. Benjamin Franklin, *The Autobiography of Benjamin Franklin.* (Mineola NY: Dover Publications), 1996, 64–74.

35. Koch, 77.

36. Emmet Kennedy, *A Cultural History of the French Revolution.* (New Haven: Yale University Press), 1989, 14.

37. "La libre communication des pensées et des opinions est un des droits les plus précieux de l'Homme: tout Citoyen peut donc parler, écrire, imprimer librement, sauf à répondre de l'abus de cette liberté, dans les cas déterminés par la Loi."

38. Sarah Maza, "The Rose-Girl of Salency: Representations of Virtue in Prerevolutionary France." *Eighteenth-Century Studies*, (Vol. 22, No. 3, Spring, 1989), 397, www.jstor.org/stable/2738894.

39. Ibid., 408.

40. Ibid, 409.

41. Jeremy L. Caradonna, "The Monarchy of Virtue: The "Prix de Vertu" and the Economy of Emulation in France, 1777–91," *Eighteenth-Century Studies.* (Vol. 41, No. 4 (Summer, 2008), 445, doi: 10.1353/ecs.0.0009.

42. Ibid., 447.

43. "Quelles couleurs ! quelle variété! quelle richesse d'objets et d'idées! Cet homme a tout, excepté la vérité." Denis Diderot, *Œuvres esthétiques* (Paris: Edition Garnier Frères), 1968, 449.

44. "Monsieur Fragonard, cela est diablement fade." Ibid., 476.

45. Jean-Baptiste Greuze. *Web Gallery of Art*. www.wga.hu/html/g/greuze/curse2.html.

46. Diderot, 549.

47. Ibid.

48. Ibid., 481.

49. Benjamin West. *WebMuseum, 2002*. www.ibiblio.org/wm/paint/auth/west/.

50. *Creating and Image of Peace*. The State Museum of Pennsylvania. www.statemuseumpa.org/Potamkin/creating/index.htm.

51. *Paul Revere House*. www.paulreverehouse.org/bio/bio.shtml.

52. John Singleton Copley. *WebMuseum, 2002*. www.ibiblio.org/wm/paint/auth/copley/.

53. Museum of Fine Arts, Boston MA. Notes on the engraving. Paul Revere's teapot is displayed next to the portrait. The engraving of the Boston Massacre is shown nearby.

54. *Charles Wilson Peale's Museum*. The Academy of Natural Sciences of Drexel University. www.ansp.org/museum/jefferson/otherPages/peale_museum.php.

55. Lee Quinby, "Thomas Jefferson, The Virtue of Aesthetics and the Aesthetics of Virtue," *The American Historical Review*, (Vol. 87, No. 2, Apr., 1982), 338, www.jstor.org/stable/1870123.

56. Ibid., 354.

57. Koch, 393.

BIBLIOGRAPHY

Adams, John. *The Adams-Jefferson Letters*. Chapel Hill: The University of North Carolina Press, 1988.

Alexander, Hartley Burr. "Rousseau and Political Humanitarianism." *The Journal of Philosophy, Psychology and Scientific Methods*, Vol. 14, No. 22 (Oct. 25, 1917): 589–611. www.jstor.org/stable/2940308.

Caradonna, Jeremy L. "The Monarchy of Virtue: The "Prix de Vertu" and the Economy of Emulation in France, 1777–91." *Eighteenth-Century Studies*. Vol. 41, No. 4 (Summer, 2008): 443–458. doi: 10.1353/ecs.0.0009.

Crisafulli, Allessandro S. "Montesquieu's Story of the Troglodytes." In *Charles-Louis de Secondat, Baron de Montesquieu*, edited by David Carrithers, 41–61. Surrey, England and Burlington Vt: Ashgate, 2009.

Copley, John Singleton. www.ibiblio.org/wm/paint/auth/copley.

Declaration of Rights of the State of Virginia. www.archives.gov/exhibits/charters/virginia_declaration_of_rights.html.

Diderot, Denis. *Œuvres esthétiques*. Paris: Edition Garnier Frères, 1968.

Diderot, Denis et Jean d'Alembert. *Encyclopédie*. www.alembert.free.fr/index.php?option=com_content&view=article&id=45&Itemid=27.

Franklin, Benjamin. *The Autobiography of Benjamin Franklin*. Mineola, NY: Dover Publications, 1996.

———. *Poor Richard's Almanack*. www.richhall.com/poor_richard.htm.

Furet, François and Mona Ozouff. *A Critical Dictionary of the French Revolution*. Cambridge MA: The Belknap Press of Harvard University Press, 1989.

Greuze, Jean-Baptiste. www.wga.hu/html/g/greuze/curse2.html.

Grimsely, Ronald. "The Idea of Nature in the *Lettres Persanes*." In *Charles-Louis de Secondat, Baron de Montesquieu*, edited by David Carrithers, 27–40. Surrey, England and Burlington Vt: Ashgate, 2009.

Henry, Patrick. "Voltaire as Moralist." *Journal of the History of Ideas*, Vol. 38, No. 1 (Jan.–Mar., 1977): 141–146. www.jstor.org/stable/2708846.

Hoyt, Nellie S. and Thomas Cassirer. *Encyclopedia*. New York: The Bobbs-Merrill Company, 1965.

Kennedy, Emmet. *A Cultural History of the French Revolution*. New Haven: Yale University Press, 1989.

Keohane, Nannerl O. "Virtuous Republics and Glorious Monarchies." In *Charles-Louis de Secondat, Baron de Montesquieu*, edited by David Carrithers, 217–230. Surrey, England and Burlington Vt: Ashgate, 2009.

Koch, Adrienne. *The American Enlightenment*. New York: Braziller, 1968.

Maza, Sarah. "The Rose-Girl of Salency: Representations of Virtue in Prerevolutionary France." *Eighteenth-Century Studies*, Vol. 22, No. 3, Special Issue: The French Revolution in Culture (spring, 1989): 395–412. www.jstor.org/stable/2738894.

Montesquieu. *De l'esprit des lois*. Paris: Garnier, 1961.

———. *Pensées et fragments inédits, Tome 1*. (Bordeaux: Gounouilhou), 1899. books.google.com/books?id=TNRcAAAAMAAJ&printsec=frontcover&dq=montesquieu+pensees&source=bl&ots=RseuZsNkBb&sig=YTuxvLt5y1rkbtLtnPRagkgqxo&hl=en&ei=dFF2TduQOa2Q0QGA9sXcBg&sa=X&oi=book_result&ct=result&resnum=2&ved=0CB0Q6AEwATge#v=onepage&q&f=false.

———. *Lettres Persanes*. Paris: Garnier-Flammarion, 1964.

Newcomb, Robert. "Benjamin Franklin and Montaigne." *Modern Language Notes*, Vol. 72, No. (7 Nov., 1957): 489–49. www.jstor.org/stable/3043511?seq=2.

Nicollier, Pascal. *Déclaration des droits de l'homme et du citoyen, with commentary*. Fribourg, 1995. www.liberte.ch/wp-content/uploads/ddhc.pdf.

Oake, Roger B. "Montesquieu's Religious Ideas." *Journal of the History of Ideas*. Vol. 14, No. 4 (Oct., 1953): 548–560. www.jstor.org/stable/2707701.

Peale, Charles Wilson. www.ansp.org/museum/jefferson/otherPages/peale_museum.php.

Quinby, Lee. "Thomas Jefferson, The Virtue of Aesthetics and the Aesthetics of Virtue." *The American Historical Review*, Vol. 87, No. 2 (Apr., 1982): 337–356. www.jstor.org/stable/1870123.

Revere, Paul. www.paulreverehouse.org/bio/bio.shtml.

Rodmell, Graham E. "A Quaker Prisoner in France (1756)." *Eighteenth-Century Studies*, Vol. 7, No. 1 (Autumn, 1973): 78–92. www.jstor.org/stable/3031613.

Rousseau, Jean-Jacques. *Du contrat social et autres œuvres politiques*. Paris: Classiques Garnier, 1975.

———. *Emile. (Profession de foi du vicaire savoyard)*. Paris: Garnier-Flammarion, 1966.

State Museum of Pennsylvania, *Creating an Image of Peace*. www.statemuseumpa.org/Potamkin/creating/index.htm.

Virginia Declaration of Rights. www.virginiamemory.com/online_classroom/shaping_the_constitution/doc/religious_freedom.

Voltaire. *Romans et contes*. Paris: Garnier-Flammarion, 1966.

West, Benjamin. www.wga.hu/art/w/west/penn.jpg.

CHAPTER THREE

Civilizing the National Discourse: The Liberal Arts As Conversation in John Henry Newman's *Idea of a University*

Barbara C. Lonnquist

Turn to improved life and you will find *conversation* in all its forms the medium of something more than an idle pleasure, indeed, a very active agent in circulating and forming the opinions, tastes, and feelings of a whole people.

John Henry Newman
Idea of a University

No passion is stronger in the breast of man than the desire to make others believe as he believes. Nothing so cuts at his happiness and fills him with rage as that another rates low what he prizes high. Whigs and Tories, Liberal party and Labour party—for what do they battle except their own prestige. It is not love of truth but desire to prevail that sets quarter against quarter and makes parish desire the downfall of parish.

Virginia Woolf
Orlando

The place of education is a special province within a society, a place where freedom of inquiry and thought occur and are protected and where—it must be said—the social and political context plays an important role by defining the limits and expectations of the learning process.

Edward Said
"On the University"

The American political landscape of late has been marked by an increasingly divisive and at times rancorous partisanship. In the summer preceding the 2010 midterm elections, a number of town hall meetings (the folksy title of which might suggest an amicable or at least respectful exchange of thoughts between citizens and legislators) degenerated into shouting matches and in a few cases "Tea Party" activists carried not only banners of protest (most notably the Gadsden flag with its coiled snake and legend "DON'T TREAD ON ME") but weapons as well. The explosive rhetoric witnessed in those grass roots gatherings has also infiltrated the halls of congress. Congressional outbursts are not uncommon in the history of the republic, but on two separate occasions, when the president addressed congress, a legislator and a high judicial figure respectively transgressed the customary bounds of restraint attending such formal gatherings by publically challenging the veracity of the American president. In an NPR report on the emergence of candidates for the 2012 presidential election, one commentator suggested that former Governor and Ambassador to China, Jon Huntsman, who had been dubbed "the civility candidate," could perhaps not answer the desire for "red meat" in certain districts of the country. The present climate of polarization is sustained by media outlets that cater to one political point of view and amplified by proliferating sources of rapid, continuous and often unregulated expression of opinion producing what could be described as a culture of spontaneous verbal combustion. Such incivility poses a threat to the very notion of a civil national discourse. Without sounding too pessimistic, it may be fair to say that a lack of civility has infected almost every level of public discourse from ordinary conversation between citizens to electronic messages in the workplace to public postings in blogs and social media.

The tragic shooting of a congresswoman as she met with her constituents (including a young child who was fatally wounded) in Tuscon in January of 2011, led to a temporary reprieve from over-heated political rhetoric and a moment of communal self-examination. After the speeches and memorial services, however, business as usual has tended to resume (as seen in the debt ceiling crisis in the summer of 2011 that is the background against which I write). Questions about the civility of our exchange, how we converse with one another—like those about the conditions and future of honest journalism—remain at the heart of America's ability to maintain a functioning democracy. "The waning sense of common purpose that comes with a climate of prolonged discord," as Michael Lacey has described in another context, not only threatens national progress but undermines the nature of what it means to be human (2).

The university has traditionally served as *the* pre-eminent site for the cultivation of a civil discourse and the interrogation of the effects of language upon the life of a people. From medieval times, the study of the nature and operations of language has been central to the liberal arts. In the medieval university, the seven liberal (as opposed to manual) arts were divided into the "trivium," or verbal arts (grammar, rhetoric and logic or dialectics) and the "quadrivium" or mathematical arts (arithmetic, geometry, music and astronomy). As the term "artes liberalis" (derived from Latin "liber" or free) suggests, the ability to reason was thought to "free the individual from the chaos of irrationality" ("The Medieval University"). In nineteenth-century England a liberal education served to create a national identity and functioned in David Harvey's words, as "the guardian of a national culture" ("University, Inc.") Victorian thinkers such as Matthew Arnold (dubbed England's "Apostle of Culture") who defended the liberal humanist tradition, and John Henry Newman, the author of *The Idea of a University*, which many critics agree remains to this day one of the most resonant sources for English speakers discussing the role of higher education, viewed the liberal arts tradition as an antidote to the cultural erosion (or "philistinism," as Arnold referred to it), spurred by the forces of industry and capitalist materialism. The goal of what Newman called a "liberal" or "philosophical" education was not simply an abstraction or a particular form of knowledge, rather it conjured an "intellectual culture" that was embodied in individuals with a certain "habit of mind" or "inward endowment." As Bill Readings has noted in *The University in Ruins*, liberal education for Newman was "figured in the life of a gentleman rather than as an idea" (77). Newman's conclusion that the liberally educated person is ultimately "useful" to society because he "elevates the tone of the whole" recuperates the medieval understanding of the trivium or verbal arts as the useful arts—an understanding often reversed in the modern opposition between culture and science that grew out of the nineteenth century.

Arnold's and Newman's resistance to utilitarian visions of education, limited to the acquisition of skills that have immediate practical applications or "market value" in their own new world of science and technology seems prescient of the current commodification of higher learning in American universities, which, having lost the government subsidies so available in the aftermath of World War II, have increasingly adopted a corporate model. In this competitive "market place," colleges, especially smaller liberal arts institutions, turn to marketing firms to "brand" their product to recruit students for economic survival (or in some cases to insure a population fitted to a specific ideological niche). In "The Post-Welfare State University," Jeffrey Williams notes that as government support has waned, forcing universities into financial partnerships with corporate business, higher education in America has taken on "a tone of realpolitik" that dismisses traditional notions of the centrality of the humanities as out of touch (205). The danger of this, I would suggest, is not simply that fewer people will have read *Moby Dick* from beginning to end or be able to quote Shakespeare in appropriate ritual moments (although I value both) but that the diminishment of the liberal arts "rags" the very fabric of a rational and humane discourse, necessary for the survival of a democracy. In *Not for Profit: Why Democracy Needs the Humanities*, (2010), legal scholar Martha Nussbaum, echoes the concerns of Newman and Arnold and warns that "nations and systems of education" who "in a thirst for profit" discard the liberal arts as "useless frills" in order "to stay competitive in a global market may produce a generation of useful machines, rather than complete citizens who can think for themselves, criticize tradition, and understand the significance of another person's suffering and achievement" (2).

In *The University in Ruins* (1996), Bill Readings laments the replacement of what he termed Newman's "University of Culture" with the "University of Excellence," a term Readings deems empty of any real "idea" of learning and signifying the replacement of thought with consumerist skills. Following Readings, South-African scholar Reingold Nethersole has more recently observed that "the very institutional space inhabited by thought" in the university is now "being curtailed by financial considerations" (30). As with other educational theorists who have charted the shift from a university of culture envisioned by Kant and Newman, Nethersole estimates the impact of a "positivism of statistically calculable productivity in a global economy" on higher education that is reduced to the "skilling" of "'learners' for a particular workplace"(31). Without denying the necessary evolution of educational objectives in a world with "an ever expanding planetary horizon," Nethersole interrogates the implications of seeing that world solely in economic terms. He focuses in particular on the impact of the "rapid erosion of the space and status of the humanities"—specifically of literary criticism and theory, which, it must be said, occupies the very "place" in the university for the analysis of social "discourses." Moreover, relative to the purpose of this essay, Nethersole contours his discussion of the erosion of the humanities within the metaphor of a (lost) "conversation." He adopts the German term *"Gesprache"* a word connoting "dialogism," taken from a poem by Holderline: "Seit ein Gesprache wir sind/Und horen konnen voneinander" ("since we are in conversation/and can hear from each other"). Nethersole sees the intellectual conversation that has been lost in Readings' "University of Excellence" as performing the central and ethical "work" of the university because it offers a necessary, communal meditation upon our "being and acting" in the world (31–32).

One can see how in an economic landscape where students become consumers, who, in David Harvey's words "noisily proclaim their rights" ("University, Inc.") and faculty are viewed as "cost factors" in the purveyance of a "product," the customer of retail education is of a piece with the consumer of retail politics—both of whom increasingly ask what is in it for them. Bottom line concerns with finance are, however, not the sole obstacle to authentic conversation within the university. One of the effects of the market retailing of higher education in the U.S. has been the emergence of colleges founded in the last forty years that have (like proliferating cable news outlets) fitted themselves within an ideological niche intended for a specific target audience. It is perhaps not accidental that many of the colleges in this category have defined themselves in response to the "culture wars" that have riddled the nation (and the Churches) in these years. A simple Google search reveals websites that can direct prospective students (or their parents) to colleges "friendly to home schooled students" (e.g. one university in Virginia identifies itself as founded for Christian home-school students) or conservative religious groups (e.g. "faithful" Catholics). A growing number of self-identified "neo-orthodox" Catholic colleges advertised as "solidly loyal" to the magesterium (teaching authority) of the Church present themselves as an alternative to the perceived secularization of older, established Catholic universities who often attract a more diverse population and who offer what their critics view as a "liberalized" curriculum, a term that is shorthand for either "cultural studies" (gender, race or postcolonial studies) or a religious studies program that foregrounds Catholic social teaching and service as opposed to a strict neo-scholastic, doctrinal focus. In some cases the claim of an "orthodox liberal arts" curriculum can signify a narrowly defined or highly selective version of the liberal arts (e.g. one such college advertises a "devoutly Catholic classical Great Books program"). Such neo-orthodoxy is seen by some as a response to a crisis of authority in post-Vatican II, American Catholicism.[1]

The university, however, as its name suggests—and did to Newman—has traditionally been by definition the site that offered the possibility of a diverse, intellectual community, of people from varied backgrounds, perspectives and "discourses" and where students could participate in a mutual exchange not only of information but of lived experience and world view. Participating in that conversation was to be "in training" so to speak for one's role in the world. Newman's celebration of the unified character of a university arising out of just such plurality strikes the contemporary reader as surprisingly relevant:

> It is seeing the world on a small field with little trouble; for the pupils or students come from very different places and with widely different notions, and there is much to generalize, much to adjust, much to eliminate, there are interrelations to be defined, and conventional rules to be established, in the process by which the whole assemblage is molded together and gains one tone and one character (*Idea* 111).

The packaging of colleges for a more homogeneous student body (a move analogous in some ways to political gerrymandering for a monolithic voting block) impoverishes the intellectual "gesprache" of the university, creating the cultural equivalent to what University of Texas economist, Daniel Hamermesh, writing in the *Chronicle of Higher Education* about the financial landscape of private universities has referred to as "gated communities" (45). Such partitioning at the university level has serious implications for the maintenance of a civil national discourse and reinforces the ideological divides that ultimately threaten the common good.

One irony in this fracturing of Catholic institutions of higher education is that some of the current critics of mainstream Catholic universities (judged too ecumenical in population or thought) have claimed Newman as the model for their neo-orthodoxy.[2] My attempt here is not to deny the right of any university to determine its identity, nor is it to argue for what critics of pluralism label as "moral relativism"; rather, what I propose is a balanced re-reading of Newman's vision for a "Catholic" university and "universal knowledge" with attention to the discursive

terrain in which he composed *The Idea of a University* and to his recurring evoca-
tion of the image of "conversation" throughout the discourses as something more
than simply a literary (unitive or decorative) device in discourses composed over
time, but a constant that is constitutive of his philosophy of knowledge and his understanding of the ethical calling of a university to help elevate the national discourse and thus aid the health and progress of society.

MYRIAD MINDED NEWMAN

The complexity of Newman's thought as it is reflected not only in his notions of a
liberal education but throughout the body of his work reveals him to be at once a
man of his time and a prophetic thinker whose ideas transcended his historical moment; such complexity and in particular Newman's demonstrated ability to re-
think, to question even his own premises and come to new conclusions defies easy
or facile categorization. Nor should one forget how his ideas vexed the authorities
of his day. That said, scholars do generally agree that Newman was not a "liberal"
in the sense in which he used the term in reference to the liberal Protestantism of
his day, which emphasized private subjectivity ("sentiment and taste") in opposition to the dogmas of the Christian Church. As the Oxford theologian and
renowned biographer of Newman, Father Ian Kerr points out, just as Newman opposed a false conservatism, he similarly decried an erroneous liberalism in religion
which he defined as "the doctrine that there is no positive truth in religion but that
one creed is as good as another"("The Mind of Newman"). Newman's bedrock
faith in the existence of revealed truth, which he gradually came to see as residing
in the Church of Rome, does not mean, however, that his thinking was in any way
monolithic. Newman was no positivist, but neither was he an apologist for what
Michael Lacey and others have more recently called "ecclesiastical positivism"
(Lacey 8). The same Newman who famously pledged (in reply to ultramontane
extremism) "to Conscience first and to the Pope afterwards" was also the author
of the philosophical *Grammar of Ascent* written as Cambridge historian Eamon
Duffy notes, "in the midst of the furor over papal infallibility" (64).

Both in his lifetime as a leading force in the Oxford Movement, formed in the
1830s by Oxford trained clerics working for reform within the Anglican Church,
and after his conversion to Catholicism in 1845, John Henry Newman presented a
complex and often controversial figure who inspired both hagiography and critique. Newman's conversion (which Prime Minister Gladstone deemed a calamity)
was obviously a "trophy" for Rome earning him a kind of "celebrity" (Duffy 64).
As a thinker Newman was something of a provocateur, whose writings were
viewed with suspicion not only by Anglicans but by the Catholic Church as well.
Newman's Tract 90, the last of "Tracts for the Times," the series of pamphlets published between 1833 and 1841 by members of the Oxford Movement (also thus
known as the "Tractarians") effectively ended the Oxford Movement when it ges-
tured toward Rome somewhat too emphatically for the Anglican Bishop of Oxford,

by attempting to reconcile the Thirty-Nine Articles of the Church of England with Catholic doctrine. On the other hand, Newman's 1845 *Essay on the Development of Christian Doctrine*, which described the shaping of ideas and beliefs as an evolutionary, dynamic phenomenon preserving the essence of truth in the flux of history, earned the skepticism of Rome. According to Duffy, such "nuanced historicism" in the face of Rome's "unchanging authority" (along with Newman's later opposition to the ultramontane faction pushing for the declaration of papal infallibility, the English part of which was headed by Edward Manning, the Archbishop of Westminster a fellow convert to Catholicism) cast Newman in Duffy's words as "half-hearted at best, treacherous at worst" (64).[3]

In contemporary Catholicism, Newman has been viewed simultaneously as the prophet of "The Second Vatican Council" sometimes called "Newman's Council" (Nash 14) and the inspiration of a post-Vatican II neo-orthodoxy. In 1975, addressing an academic symposium of Newman scholars in Rome, Pope Paul VI recalled that Newman who "prophetically foresaw" the uncertainties of the modern world, was often "misunderstood and misinterpreted" in his own time. The Pope also asserted that Newman's ideas, especially with regard to ecumenism and the role of the laity, became the very subjects discussed by the Fathers of Vatican II, and he honored Newman by calling the council "Newman's hour" (Newman Reader.org). Those Catholics old enough to remember Vatican II, can likely recall the emergence of the word "dialogue" into the ecclesiastical and pastoral discourse of the day, a fulfillment of Newman's idea a century before that the laity should be in conversation with the Vatican. Conversely, Pope John Paul II's hailing of Newman as a model of "faith and reason" has been taken up by men who identify themselves within a position of post-Vatican II neo-orthodoxy (described above).[4] It is thus with some trepidation that one invokes Newman not simply because of his prodigious reading, intellect and output, but because of the tendency at times to employ—or even colonize—Newman in the service of a specific ideology.

Two readers of Newman in the past decade or so, who emphasize Newman's sense of balance, are the respected literary scholars Carol Christ and Edward Said, both of whom share a keen interest in the state of higher education. Their readings of Newman in a historical and global context respectively, delineate the largeness and universality of his thought. In "The Victorian University and Our Own," Carol Christ, a noted Victorian scholar and president of Smith College, affirms Newman's lasting significance for our own current discussions of the role of the liberal arts. Christ argues that Newman advocated not only for knowledge as a positive end in itself (a counter to the utilitarian views emerging in his day) but for a universal knowledge that is produced in the interaction (what I am calling a "conversation") among the various branches of knowledge. Christ locates Newman's discourses in the context of nineteenth-century debates in England about the role of education, the most famous of which were the public lectures by Thomas Huxley(also known as "Darwin's bulldog"), who advocated for science education, and Matthew Arnold, who vigorously defended the "value of studying humane letters."

Christ notes that "despite the influence that Matthew Arnold's ideas had upon the shaping of the curriculum in nineteenth-century America (Arnold brought his lecture "On Literature and Science to America in 1883 including to Smith College), they have aged less well than those of Huxley or Newman" partly because, as she sees it, Arnold in attempting to subordinate the sciences to the humanities, "sustains a sense of two oppositional cultures that colleges and universities have increasingly sought to bridge and integrate" (288). Newman's *Idea of a University* by contrast remains "the most comprehensive and influential" (289)—and I would add, influential because of its comprehensiveness.

Christ cites Newman's statement that "students profit by learning from a faculty who 'zealous' for their own sciences and rivals of each other are brought, by *familiar intercourse* and for the sake of intellectual peace, to adjust together the claims and relation of their respective subjects of investigation" (qtd. in Christ 290, emphasis mine). For Newman, "Individual disciplines grow by completing, correcting and balancing one another (Christ 290, *Idea* 75). For Newman the "liberal" in "liberal arts" signifies an intellectual generosity, which allows for a polite interchange of possibly colliding ideas within a university environment that Newman imaged as needing a degree of "elbow room" (Christ 290). Newman's concern for what he called "the whole circle" was made with particular force in regard to the inclusion of theology in the curriculum. It is important to recognize that at the time Newman was composing the discourses, theology was not part of the English university curriculum (in England or Ireland). It was a radical curricular change at the time to include Theology as "a branch of knowledge" (the topic of his second discourse). When Newman asserts "certainly the very name of University is inconsistent with restrictions of any kind" (*Idea* 25) he was defending theology as a legitimate subject. However, unlike Arnold who pushed for the superiority of one branch of knowledge (humane letters), Newman places theology in conversation with other forms of knowledge. Newman's vision of the interplay between the branches of knowledge, the way in which they balance and exert pressure on each other in the pursuit of truth, suggests the university itself as a model for those habits of mind that form the character of the educated person capable of "comparison, discrimination and judgment of relationship" (Christ 289).

Newman's insistence that developing the power of "judgment" was a key component of a liberal education enabled him to defend freedom in scientific pursuit, as outlined in "On Christianity and Scientific Investigation." Here Newman affirms that inquirer who

> confident from the impulse of a generous faith, that however the line of his investigation may swerve now and then, and vary to and fro in its course, or threaten momentary collision or embarrassment with any other department of knowledge, theological or not, yet, if he lets it alone, it will come home, because truth never can really be contrary to truth. . . . Unless he is at liberty to investigate on the basis and according to the peculiarities of his science, he cannot investigate at

all. It is the very law of the human mind in its inquiry after and acquisition of truth to make its advances by a process which consists of many stages and is circuitous. (*Idea* 229–230)

Newman's defense of freedom of inquiry ran counter to Catholic fears of science in the aftermath of Darwin and echoes perhaps the evolution of Newman's own conversion as described in *Apologia Pro Vita Sua*. Furthermore, his confidence that despite temporary errors, freedom of investigation leads ultimately to truth rests not only on taking the long view (a Darwinian concept) but on faith in the convergence and cooperation of many minds: "It is not often the fortune of any one man to live through an investigation; the process is one of not only many stages but many minds. What one begins another finishes; and a true conclusion is at length worked out by the co-operation of independent schools and the perseverance of successive generations" (*Idea* 230).

Newman's belief in the potential of earnest and judicious dialogue (whether in science, theology or culture) rests on his understanding of liberally educated persons as those who have been "taught to see things as they are, to go right to the point, to disentangle a skein of thought, to detect what is sophistical and discard what is irrelevant" (*Idea* 126). Such discrimination is central to Newman's understanding of rhetorical training as leading to a habit of mind that is more than mere skill; rather, it is a kind of intellectual virtue. "A university training," he asserts, "is the great ordinary means to a great but ordinary end; it aims at raising the intellectual tone of a society, at cultivating the public mind, at purifying the national taste, at supplying true principles to popular enthusiasm" (125). Reading this in the light of current populist enthusiasms in the United States, some of which demonstrate scant respect for knowledge, one can appreciate even more Newman's commitment to intellectual and civil discourse as vital to society. The educated person Newman concludes is one who has acquired the "art" of conversation, who has learned:

> how to accommodate himself to others, how to throw himself into their state of mind, how to bring before them his own, how to influence them, how to come to an understanding with them, how to bear with them. He is at home in any society, he has common ground with any class, he knows when to speak and when to be silent. He is able to converse; he is able to listen. He can ask a question pertinently, and gain a lesson seasonably when he has nothing to impart himself . . . (*Idea* 126)

It is significant that Newman's *Idea of a University* was itself produced in a series of "discourses" to an audience addressed throughout as "Gentlemen." Christ notes, however, that Newman's emphasis "on the ideal gentleman" can "obscure the fact that his university project is in fact a democratizing one" (290). This is nowhere made more clearly than in Newman's "Address to the Evening Classes" (i.e. the working class men of Dublin) in whose "advancement," he says, "Ireland is advanced." Unlike Matthew Arnold, who famously slighted the "Celtic spirit" in his writings on Ireland,[5] Newman saw Ireland as having a role in the future of trans-Atlantic communication between Europe and America and he praised the Irish as a "people of great natural abilities, keen-witted, original and subtle" ("Evening Classes" 484–485.) Most remarkable perhaps in the context of defining liberal education as conversation is Newman's urging of these young evening students not to let knowledge "be passively received" but actively engaged: he bid them "to meet" what comes to you and enter into that "catechetical instruction which consists in a form of *conversation* between your lecturer and you" (489, my emphasis). Given the nature of catechetical practice in nineteenth-century English public schools and in the Irish Church, a form of education, whose purpose was to limit inquiry and thus control the knowledge imparted to a perceived underclass (e.g. the laborer's child or the Catholic laity respectively) by framing instruction within a rigidly scripted recitation of questions and answers (demonstrated memorably in Charles Dickens' 1857 novel *Hard Times*), Newman's reformulation of "catechetical instruction" as a mutual "conversation," between student and instructor—and its implicit sense of intellectual justice—is nothing less than stunning.[6]

Although Newman never participated in the politics of some of his fellow Anglican clergymen whose "socialist theology" led to active involvement in social labor movements or the struggle for material justice (e.g. perhaps the best known example is Charles Kingsley, who like Newman was a novelist and clergyman).[7] Newman's educational practice can be seen as a form of intellectual justice. The critic of our own day, who has best read the implicit connection in Newman's writing between liberal education and justice, is the late Edward Said, who is considered, as Ferial J. Ghazoul, the editor of *Edward Said and Critical Decolonization*, has noted, "one of the most respected academic scholars in the field of literary criticism and cultural studies" and a "charismatic Third World intellectual" (7). In Said's posthumously published essay in this collection, "On the University," an address delivered in 1999, to the students of the American University in Cairo, Said argued for the university as a "hallowed place" where "intellectual and moral values" are joined within "inquiry, discussion and exchange" (28). Said, a Palistinian-American, who spent his teaching career at Columbia University, invokes Newman in this address as not only the one who "best defined the university," but, importantly for Said, did so in a way entirely free of any suggestion of "coercion" or "dominance" (29–30). Said's advocacy for academic freedom in an Egypt still governed by the repressive Mubarak regime and a university system, in which academic freedom was further menaced by fundamentalist forces, echoes to some degree Newman's own position a century before as he faced the constraints imposed by a clerical culture that combined Irish resistance to Newman, the Englishman, and Vatican skepticism about Newman, the progressive, as Colin Barr has detailed in his revealing study of the ecclesiastical background against which both Newman and Archbishop Cullen struggled in the project of founding a Catholic University in Ireland.[8]

Like Carol Christ, Said affirms the "synthetic wholeness" of Newman's vision and specifically celebrates Newman's claim that "education should *map out the universe*" (Said's emphasis 31). Newman's expectation that the academy should develop the "power of viewing many things at once as one whole, of referring them severally to their true place in the universal system, of understanding their respective values, and determining their mutual dependence" is, Said asserts, of "special relevance to the fraught political situations of conflict, the unresolved tensions and social as well as moral disparities constitutive to the world of today" (31). Newman's view of universal knowledge, as Said sees it, offers an antidote to both repressive nationalism and religious militancy. Said invokes Newman against the notion that "[Arab students] should in a university read only what is considered safe and orthodox," which Said warns, will ultimately "prevent us from participating in the march of humanity. . . . Not to deal with that whole—which is in fact a contemporary version of the whole referred to by Newman as a true enlargement of mind" is, for Said, not only to lack "academic freedom" but to forfeit "our claim as seekers after justice" (32).

Just as Newman imagined young Irishmen coming from the towns and villages of Ireland to reflect and reshape their own experience through an intellectual exchange that would balance differing perspectives, Said enjoined the Arab students to become intellectual travelers: "to discover and travel among other selves, other identities, other varieties of the human adventure" in order to "transform what might be conflict, or contest, or assertion into reconciliation, mutuality, recognition, creative interaction"(33). In Newman's address on "Christianity and Scientific Investigation," he enjoined "religious writers, jurists, economists, physiologists, chemists, geologists and historians to go on quietly and in a *neighborly way*" with "full faith" in the "the consistency of that multiform truth which they share between them" (465).

Although Said acknowledges the "western" limitations of Newman's world view as a nineteenth-century Englishman, he nevertheless channels and expands Newman's sense of the "neighbourly" for a new global reality. Said ends with the image of lifelong membership in the academy—i.e. Newman's university—as an invitation "to enter a ceaseless quest for principles and knowledge, liberation and finally justice" (36). In the history of Said's critical writing on imperialism in nineteenth-century literature and culture, Newman was often just barely a reference. I find it inspiring that in the late days of Said's life, as he employed his own role as a public intellectual attempting to bridge the political divides paralyzing the Middle East, he turned to Newman, the Catholic, in his speech to a largely Muslim audience.

Said notes the risks he is asking of those students. The epigraph from Newman at the head of this essay suggests, as Said does, that the march of human progress depends in part upon our ability to enter into civil conversation—to preserve an empathetic discourse, the "cor ad cor loquitur" (heart speaks to heart), of Newman's *Grammar of Assent*. Federal court judge and recipient of the University of Notre Dame "Laetare Medal," John T. Noonan has explained the link between knowledge and love as "the ability to identify with the other"(qtd. in Lacey 20). In a country where freedom of speech is a constitutional guarantee, the onus is ever more upon its citizens to preserve that privilege. A true liberal education, as Newman envisioned it, still offers, I believe, a way out of the rhetorical incivility that seems to have paralyzed our own national discourse of late.

NOTES

1. For two quite different analyses of the "crisis of authority" in the modern church see Joseph Varacelli's essay "neo-orthodoxy, the Crisis of Authority, and the Future of the Catholic Church in America" first published in *Faith and Reason* (1989) , a journal issued out of Christendom College in Virginia (one of the new "orthodox colleges described above) and a more recent collection of essays by theologians and historians, *The Crisis of Authority in Catholic Modernity* (2011), edited by Michael Lacey and Francis Oakley. Varacelli's essay (now available on-line from EWTN cable services), which seems to have been a kind of shot over the bow from the neo-orthodox movement in Catholic higher education, warns against "a distorted new Catholic knowledge class" created in the wake of Vatican II (and graduating presumably from more liberal Catholic institutions). In the "Prologue" to the latter collection of essays, Michael Lacey offers a respectful yet challenging critique of the continuing gaps between power and real authority in the church and between what the Vatican promulgates and what many Catholics actually believe. His very nuanced analysis (reflecting the depth and scope of the book) in no way advocates for a "shallow individualism" nor the freedom of an "unencumbered self" (a term he borrows) but is a plea for a more judicious—and just—exercise of power in the relations between the curia and the laity.

2. In the wake of Pope John Paul II's apostolic constitution on higher education, *Ex Corde Exclesiae* (1990), and his 2001 letter praising Newman's "remarkable synthesis of faith and reason (an echo of the Pope's own 1998 encyclical "Fides et Ratio") and most recently Benedict XVI's beatification of Newman in 2010, Newman has been held up as a model of holiness and intellect and adopted by various groups within Catholic higher education—e.g. Newman Institutes in the U.S. and Ireland and, most conspicuously perhaps, the American organization, the Cardinal Newman Society, a lay group founded in 1993, to be, as described in their website, a "public conscience for Catholic higher education." Their work often consists in monitoring courses taught on or speakers invited to Catholic campuses for their adherence to Church teaching. As I write this essay, the *Philadelphia Inquirer* reported today, (September 21, 2011) that a Catholic university in Pennsylvania "disinvited" a syndicated, Pulitzer Prize winning columnist scheduled to give a lecture on "civility" after the Cardinal Newman Society posted an objection to her appearance on its website. The Newman Society also posts a list for prospective college students of those Catholic colleges they designate as "faithful" to the magesterium (they identify only twenty-one). The current emphasis on evangelization among some conservative religionists (an approach which centers on "conversion" rather than "conversation") seems somewhat at odds with Newman's more comprehensive vision of the nature of a liberal education as he states it in his Preface to *The Idea of a University*.

3. See also Edward Jeremy Miller's op-ed (Sept.14, 2010) in the *Philadelphia Inquirer*, "The Complicated Cardinal." Miller describes some of the tensions between Newman and Manning. Newman greatly opposed Manning's push for the formal declaration of infallibility. Miller describes Newman as "a controversial figure who in his life and writings, achieved balance in matters that led others to one-sided stances. He had the utmost respect

for church authority but defended free theological investigation." Miller also reminds us that the complicated cardinal is no "plaster saint."

4. The title "Faith and Reason" interestingly hails back to the First Vatican Council (1869–1870).

5. In *Inventing Ireland*, Declan Kiberd cites for example Arnold's opposition to Irish Home Rule in which he "argued that 'the idle and imprudent Irish' could never properly govern themselves." Kiberd also notes with regard to Arnold's *The Study of Celtic Literature*, "scholars have demonstrated that even when his intention was to praise some quality in the Celt, Arnold never ceded his authority" (31).

6. Such catechetical instruction is envoked in the question and answer format of William Blake's poems "The Lamb" and "The Tyger" in *Songs of Innocence and Songs of Experience*. Dickens' novel *Hard Times* (contemporaneous with Newman's *Idea of a University*) opens with a famous caricature of such instruction. In it Mr. Gradgrind orders a young school master (significantly named "Choakumchild"): "Teach these boys and girls nothing but Facts. . . . You can only form the minds of reasoning animals upon Facts." Catechetical instruction was common in Ireland. In the *Dubliners* story "A Painful Case" (1906), James Joyce implies the lasting negative effect of the Maynooth Catechism upon the tragic figure of Mr. Duffy.

7. In his study of poverty and social reform in Victorian England, Seth Koven observes the distinction between the clerical reformers who followed the Christian socialist theology of Frederick Maurice, a Unitarian turned Anglican clergyman, and those who followed Newman and the Oxford Moment with its stress on aestheticism and the apostolic origins of the Church of England. It was Maurice who founded the Working Men's College of London in 1854, (131–133)—as Newman was forming the Catholic University of Ireland. It was the criticism of clergyman and novelist, Charles Kingsley (a friend and follower of Maurice's Christian socialism) that that prompted Newman to write *Apologia pro Vita Sua* (Eamon Duffy 64).

8. Barr's *Paul Cullen, John Henry Newman and the Catholic University of Ireland, 1845–1865* reveals the difficulties both Cullen and Newman encountered with Irish bishops who opposed the foundation. The Irish were skeptical of Cullen's choice of an Oxford Englishman as rector. Barr notes that a letter to Cullen from the vice Rector of the Irish College in Rome warned that "Dr. Newman is viewed in Rome now with jealousy" as "not quite orthodox" (71). Barr also addresses the conflicts between Newman and Cullen, one of which was likely a difference in education theory. Critics of Cullen say he envisioned a "lay seminary" (73). Barr cites historians Edward McCarron and Richard Finnegan: "Cullen sought to create a Catholic university, to promote an Irish Catholic education, while Newman sought to provide a liberal arts education to Irish Catholics" (qtd. in Barr 73).

WORKS CITED

Barr, Colin. *Paul Cullen, John Henry Newman, and the Catholic University of Ireland, 1845–1865*. Notre Dame, IN: Notre Dame UP, 2003.

Christ, Carol. "The Victorian University and Our Own." *Journal of Victorian Culture* 13.2 (2008):287–294.

Dickens, Charles. *Hard Times*. (1854). London: Penguin, 1995.

Duffy, Eamon. "Hero of the Church." *The New York Review of Books* LVII, 20. Dec. 23, 2010. 62–64.

Hamermesh, Daniel, S. "The Know–Nothing Assault on Higher Education." *The Chronicle of Higher Education* 2 Sept, 2011: A 44–45.

Harvey, David. "University, Inc." *The Atlantic Monthly* digital edition. Oct, 1998.

Kerr, Ian. "Introduction to John Henry Cardinal Newman's Biglietto Speech." *Logos: A Journal of Catholic Thought and Culture* 6.4(2003):164–169.

———. "The Mind of Newman." (www.christnedom-awake.org/pages/ianker/minofnewman.htm

Kiberd, Declan. *Inventing Ireland: The Literature of the Modern Nation*. Cambridge, MA: Harvard UP, 1995.

Koven, Seth. *Slumming: Sexual and Social Politics in Victorian London*. Princeton: Princeton UP, 2004.

Lacey, Michael, J. "Prologue." *The Crisis of Authority in Catholic Modernity*. Eds. Michael J. Lacey and Fracnis Oakley. New York: Oxford, UP, 2011. 1–20.

Lash, Nicholas. "Waiting for Dr. Newman." *America 02.3*. 1-8 Feb 2010: 13–14. Print.

"The Liberal arts Curriculum in the Medieval University." *The Medieval University.* www.csuponoma.edu/~plin/Is210/medieval_curriculum.html.

Miller, Edward Jeremy. "The Complicated Cardinal." Op-ed. *The Philadelphia Inquirer* 14 Sept.2010:A13. Print.

Nethersole, Reingard. "The Priceless Interval: Theory in the Global Interstice." *Diacritics* 31.3(2001):30–56.

Newman, John Henry. *The Idea of a University*. Ed. Frank M. Turner New Haven: Yale UP, 1996.

———. "Occasional Essays and Lectures Delivered to Member of the Catholic University." *The Idea of a University. Part II*. London: Longmans, Green and Co, 1901.

Nussbaum, Martha C. *Not for Profit: Why Democracy Needs the Humanities*. Princeton, NJ: Princeton UP, 2010.

Readings, Bill. *The University in Ruins*. Cambridge, MA: Harvard UP, 1996.

Rodgers, Ann. "College Disinvites Ellen Goodman." *The Philadelphia Inquirer* 21 Sept, 2011: B4.

Said, Edward. "On the University." *Edward Said and Critical Decolonization*. Ed. Ferial J. Ghazoul. Cairo: The American U in Cairo P, 2007.

"Tract 90." html//Supremacy and Survival: The English Reformation. blogspot.com/2011/01/tract-90-january25, 20-1841.html

Vacarelli, Joseph. "Neo-orthodoxy, the Crisis of Authority and the Future of the Catholic Church in the United States." *Faith and Reason* (1989). Reprinted courtesy EWTN Network. http://www.ewtn.com, 1997.

Williams, Jeffrey. "The Post-Welfare State University." *American Literary History* 18.1 (2006):190–216.

CHAPTER FOUR

Out of the Gutter:[1] Illness and Disability in the Graphic Narrative

Karen J. Getzen

All people, whether they like to think about it or not, and regardless of race, gender, or sexual orientation, are vulnerable to the onset of disability. This quick and profound change is rather like Clark Kent's transformation in reverse: the average Joe enters the phone booth only to emerge as a disabled man with a wheelchair instead of a fancy cape.

—Catherine Scott 311

ABSTRACT: This chapter draws on the growing body of graphic novels. An examination of David Beauchard's *Epileptic* and Al Davison's *The Spiral Cage* expand our understanding of illness and disability experience as well as how the visual and verbal grammars of the graphic novel work. I argue that our deeper understanding of illness and disability through the reading of graphic novels ultimately contributes to a more just and civil society.

ACKNOWLEDGMENT: Special thanks to Matt Getzen for his thoughtful critique.

Illness and disability narratives[2] have received a great deal of attention and some would say, legitimization, in recent years. In 1996 James Atlas, writing for *The New York Times* magazine, declared the triumph of the literary memoir and linked this moment with our "culture of confession" (2). One robust subgenre of the current memoir field addresses illness and disability.

At the same time that the shift towards confessional memoirs gained legitimization our culture became more invested in images. Footage of ground zero,

49

the incendiary photographs of Abu Ghraib, the debate about showing images of soldiers' caskets returning from Iraq, as well as our concern about making photographs of recently slain Osama bin Laden available are examples of how visual we as a culture have become. According to Whitlock, such images raise questions that are political and urgent. "We live," she suggests, "in times when attending to the relation between visual cultures and the transmission of memories of trauma and violence . . . ripple out to broader issues of visual and verbal literacy" (966). The graphic narrative makes use of these two literacies. It is perhaps not surprising then that in the midst of these cultural shifts the graphic novel[3] (henceforward referred to as the *graphic narrative*) is gaining not only acceptance, but respect.

Two graphic narratives, *The Spiral Cage* by Al Davison and *Epileptic* by David B., will be examined to explicate *how* these image texts work and *what* they bring to illness and disability studies. These have been selected because of their similarities—the portrayal of identity development in the face of illness and disability, and for their remarkable differences—their image and narrative styles as well as the form of the life story that each tells. In addition, they differ with respect to the narrator's location and place: *The Spiral Cage* is about the *author's* life with spina bifida, a severe medical condition, and *Epileptic* is about the impact of the author's *brother's* incapacitating epilepsy. Both narratives will help us see why this art form is especially suited to address the sociopolitical and personal effects of illness and disability in general but particularly in our postmodern world.

In the graphic narrative there is an array of visual considerations—including gutters, panels, drawing and lettering style, and the like, but also the narrative and what occurs between the image and the text. Versaci suggests that the graphic narrative has certain advantages over prose alone. Graphic narratives have the capacity to achieve immediate intimacy (for example, by having the an image of the author looking the reader in eye) with their reader; they provide a "secret window" (39) into characters' interior lives through the use of thought bubbles and text boxes; and these devices allow for "the disjunction between narrator and character" (39). Versaci further argues that if so much were going on in a prose story it would be incoherent, but in the graphic narrative, the use of images act as a "unifying force that allows for a more flexible first-person narrator" (41).

Graphic narratives are also effective in presenting affect. David B. claims that his work on *Epilpetic* was not about a reconstruction of events so much as about him expressing his feelings (Arnold 1). Interestingly, the graphic narrative, with its reliance on its visual and verbal grammars, has had particular success in the areas of war, illness, disability, and other traumas. In particular, illness, and I would argue disability, seem to have found a home in these comics due in part to their realistic portrayal of the complexities of illness (Chute 413). In part this is due to comics being a medium that eschews triumphalism in favor of the unsentimental. Born of comics,[4] what is most significant is the fact that in the graphic narrative "the story operates somewhere . . . between the words and the idea that's in the pictures, and in the movements between the pictures, which is the essence of what happens in a comic" (qtd. in Huyssen 77). Comics, in other words, are not a "mere hybrid of graphic arts and prose fiction, but a unique interpretation that transcends both and emerges through the imaginative work of closure" (Whitlock 968–969). In fact because graphic narratives themselves have been so marginalized until recently, they seem to be a logical arena in which marginalized people can tell their stories.

THE SPIRAL CAGE

Al Davison's *The Spiral Cage* (2003), like David B's *Epileptic*, is a black and white graphic narrative, or graphic memoir. *The Spiral Cage* recounts Davison's life until age 30. Born with the severe neuromuscular condition spina bifida,[5] which often causes paralysis, fluid build-up in the brain, and incontinence, Davison begins his early life story by expressing his gratitude that as a newborn with a serious disability his parents insisted he receive life-sustaining medical care. From there we learn about his early years in and out of hospitals for surgeries, his school years, which include being bullied because he was different, his search for meaning through the practice of martial arts and the study of Buddhism, and his relationship with his wife, Maggie. *The Spiral Cage* is a more obviously optimistic narrative about the author's life than is David B's *Epileptic*.

Davison's graphic narrative moves back and forth in time and physical and emotional development between his birth in 1960 to his relationship with Maggie in 1989. The reader is immediately presented with the complexities of his identity formation or the presentation of "multiple selves." This begins on the first page of chapter one. We see a photograph of a smiling and healthy-looking baby in the upper center but directly underneath this, in the center of the page, a drawing of Davison as an infant with tubes from his mouth, nose, and brain.[6] The reader turns the page to unexpected drawings of the adult Davison. But in addition to seeing him in adulthood, we also see him naked. He seems to almost tease the reader by showing himself on one page (10) as an adult crawling, with his underdeveloped lower legs clearly problematic and in view. On the facing page (11) we see him practicing karate with his teacher, Mitsusuke Harada. Here (Fig. 1 p. 11), Davison is muscular and disciplined. The reader is disoriented by the images of the healthy baby, the ill baby with tubes protruding, the struggling Davison with malformed legs and ankles, and the muscular, disciplined, and learned Davison who studies a martial art. He seems to challenge the reader to attempt to identify which one he is—the able-bodied or the disabled, the cute and cuddly or the malformed, the strong or the weak. He is a karate-chopping "cripple," and a cherubic looking baby who was kept alive by tubes from all orifices of his body. This functions to not only disorient the reader and to move the story forward, but to clarify that identity will be a central or at least a significant part of the narrative.

Early in the text Davison presents a scene in which he is a young child reading Mary Shelly's *Frankenstein*. He reads the well known passage of the monster

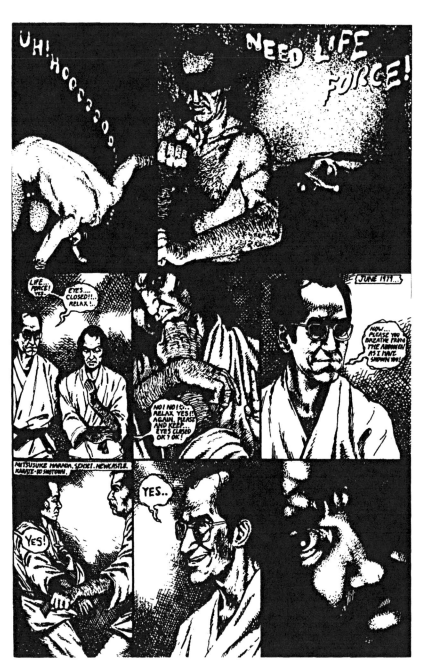

Figure 1. From SPIRAL CAGE by Al Davison, copyright 2003 by Astral Gypsy Press, Los Angeles, CA. Used with permission of the author.

viewing his reflection in a pool: ". . . when I became fully convinced that I was in reality the monster that I am, I was filled with the bitterest sensations of despondency and mortification" (42). Here, the nine even-sized panels that cover an entire page alternate between drawings of Davison as a child and drawings of the monster. This alternation suggests the impact the story has on Davison the child: the monster takes up an equivalent amount of space as Davison's drawings of himself. In the final panel the reader sees the child Davison rubbing his stomach and asking "what duz despondence and mortification mean?" (42). What we are to make of all of this is not absolutely clear, but it seems to suggest that Davison has a strong emotional response to the story of Frankenstein, even if he does not understand all of the words. He does, perhaps, understand the words ". . . that I was in reality the monster" (42) as he does not ask for clarification on their meanings. It also suggests an identification with the monster, but also the work of existential identity. Unlike those born without a serious condition like spina bifida where identity *may be* less work, for the young Davison it occupies much interior space. This is not to suggest that disability or illness is a "good thing" (*What doesn't kill you makes you stronger; God doesn't give you more than you can handle*) because it forces a great deal of life assessment and identity work, but that the complexities of identity may be amplified.

One of the most notable explorations of Davison's identity comes late in the book (Fig. 2 p. 117). At first glance we see many separate panels. There are 35 small panels of equal size that appear on a single page that include a smiling sun, the child Davison, and the strong adult Davison practicing karate or some martial art; several panels are filled with interrupted text, three are completely black, and one appears to be either a monster or Davison—it is impossible to tell which. But the specific meaning of each panel may be less significant than the effect of the overall page: Davison is many selves.[7] These panels suggest not an integration of the many selves (although it could mean this) so much as perhaps an appreciation of the many. Davison challenges the reader's possible biases by showing that he is not easily pigeonholed and at the same time he once again illustrates the complexity of identity.

Upon closer inspection, the 35 panels are superimposed on a drawing of Davison's adult face. In fact, he is looking directly into the eyes of the reader. He seems to suggest that no one panel can encapsulate him entirely. (What Art Spiegelman, author of well-known graphic narrative *Maus* means when he suggests that "the story operates somewhere . . . between the words and the idea that's in the picture" (qtd. in Huyssen 77). It also raises the possibility that although most people think about "who they are," the person who is born as "other" must address the "who am I?" question more directly and perhaps more purposefully.

The many panels on this page and the drawing of Davison that is "behind" the 35 panels, suggest hard work. Versaci argues that the self, as developed in graphic memoirs is a "rocky, uneven surface where the best writers will acknowledge the complexity of who we are . . . the self is ever shifting, socially impacted,

Figure 2. From SPIRAL CAGE by Al Davison, copyright 2003 by Astral Gypsy Press, Los Angeles, CA. Used with permission of the author.

and multifaceted" (48–49). Again, Versaci asserts that it is the graphic narrative that can effectively present multiple selves, just as Davison succeeds at doing. These many panels speak almost literally to Versaci's "uneven surface,"—the separate panels are indicative of divisions, connections, and distance as part of identity—as well as they emphasize Davison's complicated work at identity. The use of the visual combined with the verbal invite or force the reader to do what Whitlock has suggested is the essence of reading a graphic narrative: to take part in the "imaginative work of closure" (968–969). Julia Round suggests that this closure involves the reader and writer in a kind of intricate dance in which the writer tells their story *within* the panels on the page and the reader reads into the story what happens *between* the panels (200).

If identity is central to this narrative, so too is the social impact of disability as it impinges on identity formation. Davison shows and tells us directly about the experiences that underscore some of his challenges with his disability. When he was young he was ambidextrous—". . . drawing with one hand while writing a story with the other" (89). But, he goes on to say, "Certain teachers considered this a Problem, saying they were preparing me to go into the world 'as normal as possible' despite my disability, and this 'drawing problem' would make that more difficult" (89). He then adds that "one teacher started tying my left hand behind my back with my school tie" (89). Of course the irony that an ability (ambidexterity) is taken from him to "make him normal"—and thereby disable him to some extent (he can now only use one hand at a time), combined with the irony that most people might have considered the spina bifida *per se* as his "abnormality," emphasizes the tension between what is considered *normal* and what is considered *abnormal*. Making Davison solely right handed is also a way to *literally* control part of his identity: He is no longer a person who is ambidextrous; he is right handed and thus, "normal."

Later Davison dedicates an entire page to a scene of his mother having tea with a friend who refers to Davison as "poor little Alan, paralyzed and all . . . Maybe it would have been kinder to let him, well you know . . . pass away when he was born" (34).[8] But outside the window where the two women sit and have tea, Davison the child swings by on a rope with a grin on his face. He is clear-eyed and strong enough to hold not only his own weight but the weight of his casts that completely cover both legs. The juxtaposition of his mother's friend's suggestion that Davison should have been left to die at birth and the strong and smiling child at the window makes a stand against selection criteria for children born with serious birth defects and at the same time lets the reader know that Davison is not just his disability.

Davison again addresses disability and identity directly but this time as an adult. When asked by a friend, Max, what it is like to be disabled "from a purely intellectual point of view" (81) Davison responds: "Well, I'm not that intellectual . . . nor am I disabled . . . sorry" (81). He then challenges Max to a physical competition that leaves Max in pain and breathless and Davison composed and upright

(Fig. 3 p. 83). Davison then facetiously questions Max "Tell me, from a purely emotional point of view . . . how does it feel to be disabled . . . ?" (83). The answer from Max: "bloody awful right now" (83). Clearly, Davison portrays himself as not only *not* disabled, but able to fight back physically as well as verbally and intellectually. This scene captures Davison's need to defend himself and also shows the benefits of his karate work: he is not only strong and smart, but he is not disabled—even though he feels compelled to prove it.

Most provocative are drawings Davison includes of himself as an adult and naked. Many "able bodied" people can find it uncomfortable at the least and anxiety producing at the most to view what might be considered a deformed body. In addition to that a naked *and* deformed body is highly unusual for most of us to gaze at. Often we are both intrigued and repelled at the same time. According to bioethicist Leslie Fiedler, people tend to have "deep ambivalence toward fellow creatures who are perceived . . . as disturbingly deviant, outside currently acceptable physiological norms" (40). This deep social ambivalence is repeatedly addressed in both *Epileptic* and *The Spiral Cage*. But for the reader who is able to look at Davison's body, in all of its strength and impairment, what occurs is a slowly growing comfort with the images of his body.

Even more daring is Davison's inclusions near end of the book (120) of himself in bed with Maggie. She massages his misshapen feet and expresses her concern about the scar on his back from his childhood surgery that now looks irritated and red to her. The drawings are realistic and provide even more detail of his body than was available in the early part of the book where he is naked. Now it seems that the reader is ready for more. Rather than increasing any stereotypes the reader might have, we are more caught up in the love story. The spina bifida is part of that story, but it, like Davison's' practice of Karate and Buddhism and his "many selves," is only a part. Could readers be looking at these drawings purely out of curiosity—in a voyeuristic kind of way—the way one might attempt to gaze at a serious accident along the side of the highway while also wanting to look the opposite direction? Of course. But the point here is that the spina bifida has shifted out of the center and above and beyond it, Davison is a human being with human needs for meaningful relationship.

Davison uses the images to move the story forward just as he uses the prose to do the same. A key characteristic of graphic narratives is that images do not simply illustrate words any more than words simply explain or describe images. If this were the case, the phenomena of closure would not occur and perhaps not be necessary. Both the images and the narrative move the story forward. This forward movement by use of the visual is often used to "amplify the text's emotional hold on a reader" (Chute 419). This may be one reason why graphic narratives of trauma have become so popular: their ability to amplify emotion is synchronous with the fact that serious disabilities and illnesses are amplified experience.

Interestingly, Davison follows his opening pages with a page of images that *primarily* illustrate text and on which text is used to *primarily* explain the images

Figure 3. From SPIRAL CAGE by Al Davison, copyright 2003 by Astral Gypsy Press, Los Angeles, CA. Used with permission of the author.

(Fig. 4 p. 14). In the center of the page is an image of a foot, ankle, and lower leg and beside it the explanation that "his ankles are also fused . . . preventing any flexing of the feet" (14). Prior to this we learn that there is "Dislocation of left hip caused by malformation of the lateral surface of the iliac bone . . . Both femur, fibula, and tibia of both legs are severely distorted" (14). The initial graphics on this page do not truly move the story forward. Instead it is a medical record of sorts—what Frank suggests led to the notion that there is "more . . . than the medical story" (6) that must be told in our postmodern world. Here, for most of the page, Davison chooses to show the medical devoid of the emotional. He *uses* image to illustrate text and text to explain image in such a way that emotion is limited.

By the end of the page, however, Davison heightens the emotional by concluding with a panel of someone who appears to be a physician or at least someone of authority. There is a bulge on the right that could be a stethoscope protruding from the pocket, and he (it appears to be a man and in 1960 most likely would have been) holds a pointer for teaching. This apparently represents the medical profession. Immediately to the left of this panel of an authority figure is a narrative panel in which we read: "We can't even say he will survive this first operation. He is literally a 'hopeless case'" (14). In other words, Davison now uses the image to further the narrative and the narrative to develop the image. The blunted emotion that occurs over most of the page works as a kind of set up so that the reader feels the full force of emotion in those last two panels.

Well-known comic expert Alan Moore introduces *The Spiral Cage* as engendering an "uplifting sense of optimism" (3) in part because Davison "seems to have found a key to the lock of his own cage" (4). Moore acknowledges that *The Spiral Cage* addresses topics that many people do not want to talk or even think about, let alone look at. *The Spiral Cage* succeeds for many reasons, but partly because it does what graphic narratives at their best do so well—it addresses layers of identity, the complexities of disability in ways that are honest and engaging, and it effectively uses the verbal/visual grammar to move the story forward. It is a true story that is optimistic but not simple triumphalism. It is never *Pollyanish*: Throughout Davison's text he shares his own demons—"You, boy, have ideas above your station . . . You can't avoid your limitations Boy" (74–75). He could be disabled by such voices, but ultimately he finds his own voice and identity to tell his own story, to free himself of his cage.

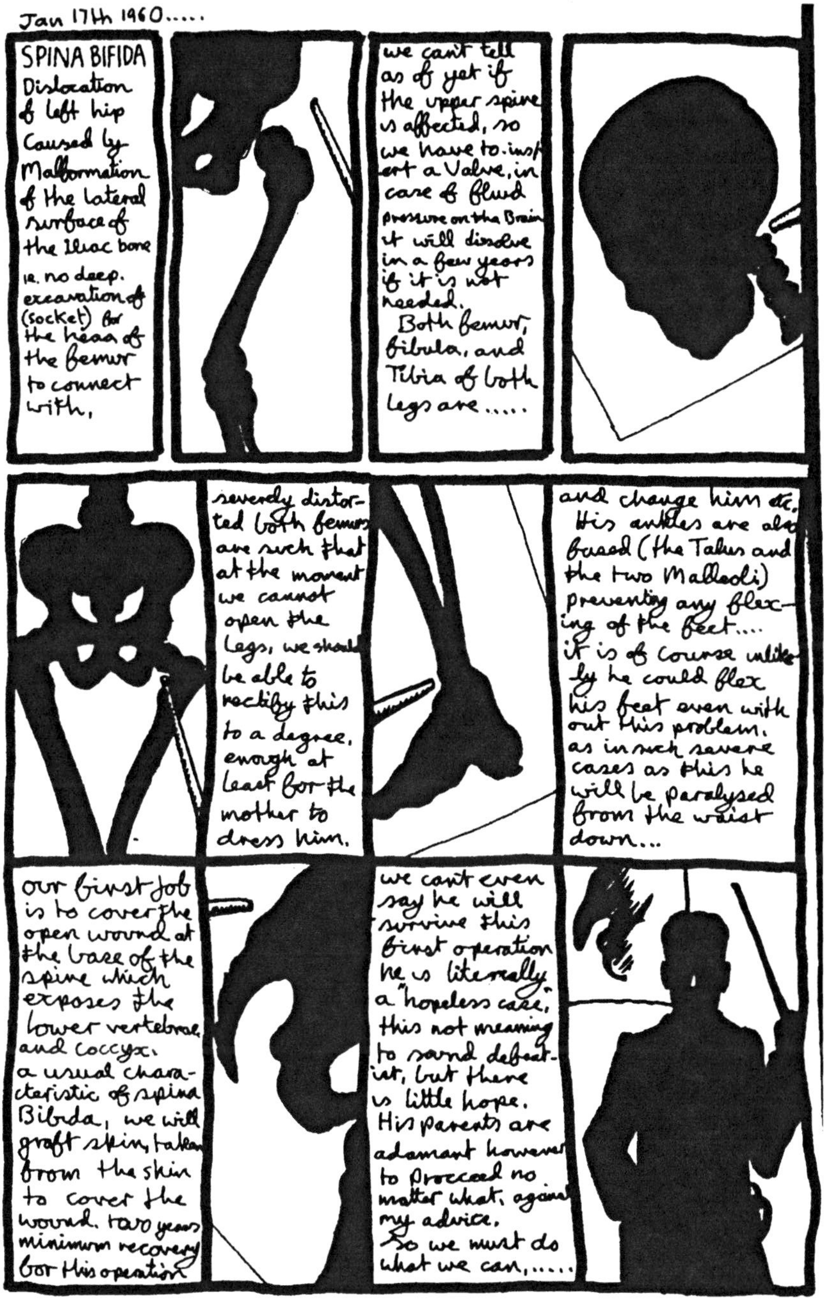

Figure 4. From SPIRAL CAGE by Al Davison, copyright 2003 by Astral Gypsy Press, Los Angeles, CA. Used with permission of the author.

EPILEPTIC

In *Epileptic*, David B. tells the story of his brother Jean-Christophe's battle with epilepsy, a brain disorder, and the severe and debilitating seizures it causes that render him unable to function. By juxtaposing real and imaginary battle scenes of war with his brother's brutal illness, the reader feels like they are experiencing their own personal war. David draws the seizures in all of their fury (Fig. 5 p. 77). In fact, *Epileptic* is known for its "dark prettiness" (Chute 423)[9] and the darkness and non-stop emotion combined with its verbal, visual, and emotional density and intensity makes it challenging to read. Battle scenes and demons represent David's emotions. His brother's illness is represented by elaborate and violent combat scenes, ghosts, snakes, skeletal-like faces, and other terrifying images. Often the very ground on which the siblings stand appears to be alive with the creatures from David's imagination.

Epileptic is not about a single event, but about a life. After a brief glimpse of their carefree, pre-epilepsy days it follows David and his brother and their family from 1964, (when David is 5 and his brother 7), through the start of the epilepsy, to 1994. It also dips back into the distant and recent past of family and world history including depictions of various wars.

Because David's parents do not trust the traditional medical community, they spend a lifetime seeking help from alternative healers—most of these involve the entire family and vary from living on a macrobiotic commune to constructing a Rosicrucian Temple in their garage, to meeting with psychics, putting David through an exorcism, to voodoo and Ouija boards. Unfortunately, none of their efforts result in any lessening of the impact of the epilepsy on Jean-Christophe or the family. As David sates, "this disease would eventually make off with all of us" (166).

Although the epilepsy does not actually "make off" with all of them, it comes close. David's parents appear to exhaust themselves in a search for a cure and Florence (the youngest of the three children) attempts suicide. Later she confides to David, "that moment was when my sadness began . . . I never got out of that period" (161). As the story progresses the threats to their lives become literal when at one point Jean-Christophe fortifies himself with all of the family's kitchen knives and in the middle of the night enters David's room with the apparent intent to stab him. However, he fails to do so and the events of their lives continue to unfold. The reader is presented with an inside view of the ravages of the illness brought on by the epilepsy but also David's attempts to tame this wild creature. In fact, David is ultimately on a life-mission or quest, but it is not until the very end of the book that the reader knows that he ultimately emerges standing on his own ground.

Unlike the optimistic opening of *The Spiral Cage*, the opening page of *Epileptic* foreshadows the difficulties ahead. It is 1994 and David and Jean-Christophe are adults (Fig. 6 p 2). We see that Jean-Christophe is bloated, missing teeth, balding and scar and scab-covered. His words seem to be forced and limited: "Don't

Figure 5. From EPILEPTIC by David B., translated by Kim Thompson, copyright © 2005 by L'Association, Paris, France. Used by permission of Pantheon Books, a division of Random House, Inc.

Figure 6. From EPILEPTIC by David B., translated by Kim Thompson, copyright © 2005 by L'Association, Paris, France. Used by permission of Pantheon Books, a division of Random House, Inc.

wanna . . . get in y'r wway . . ." (2), he says to David as they try to pass each other in the bathroom. From this one page, the reader can assume that this is not going to be what Frank would refer to as a restitution narrative. The pure restitution story goes like this: "Yesterday I was healthy. Today I'm sick, but tomorrow I'll be healthy again" (Frank 77). This is what Nicholas Regush calls "gee whiz" stories (qtd. In Frank 86) because they are about overcoming, about maintaining control, and about guaranteed outcomes. In other words, triumphalism wins out over the unsentimental, the complex, and the "messy." These narratives affirm that we can all be "fixed" and thereby leave no room for death (or serious disability) or its possibility. The problem with such narratives, of course, is that if the condition remains chronic or the person dies or becomes seriously disabled, we are stuck. This, according to Frank, is the modernist narrative type made possible and popular by the advances in medical care in the early 1900s and combined with physicians being seen as all powerful, good, and altruistic. The opening of *Epileptic* lets us know right away that this is not going to be a "pretty picture."

In fact, throughout *Epileptic* the modern world of medicine (modernism) is suspect at best. When the parents first seek out medical cure—surgery, David tells us that "Jean-Christophe is nothing more than a "case" . . . [that] will allow Professor T. to perform a brilliant operation" (44). In other words, modernism offers little. There will be no magical triumph over this illness or this situation. Frank suggests two additional types of illness narrative: the chaos narrative, and the quest narrative. In actuality these three types overlap, but for understanding each type it is best to treat them as separate entities. In addition, in real life they shift from foreground to background. I suggest that *Epileptic* is a chaos and quest narrative.

If restitution is not going to take place, what will? In fact what the reader experiences is a great deal of chaos amid a tentative quest journey that is nearly completely overpowered by the chaos. Chaos narratives lack order and present the possibility or likelihood that life will never improve. They foreground "futility, vulnerability, impotence" (Frank 97) and there is only immediacy—not reflection. It is characterized by "an incessant present" and a staccato pacing that provides a breathless "and then, and then, and then" (99). It is the narrative in which "illness and disability may turn people so far inward that they becomes black holes, absorbing energy rather than emitting illumination" (Couser 5). In other words, the incoherence that would likely make the strictly prose narrative unreadable, works in the graphic narrative. Frank provides a prose passage that represents chaos in prose form from an interview of a woman who lives with her mother who is afflicted by Alzheimer's:

> And if I'm trying to get dinner ready and I'm already feeling bad, she's in front of the refrigerator. Then she goes to put her hand on the stove and I got the fire on. And then she's in front of the microwave and then she's in front of the silverware drawer. And—and if I send her out she gets mad at me. And then it's awful. That's when I have a really, a really bad time (qtd. in Frank 99).

In *Epilpetic*, the chaos is also conveyed as an incessant present even as time shifts from past to present repeatedly. It is so incessant that the reader easily feels exhausted. There is little white space and only brief interludes when Jean-Christophe's seizures come to an inexplicable halt, but always to start again. The reader who seeks out a resting place has little success.

The third narrative type, the quest narrative, exists when a person undertakes the search for a new destination map or as Smith and Watson claim, "self-reinvention" (141). Quest narratives have a sense of purpose: I *will* reconstruct my own destination map; there is some value in this experience, even though its clarity may be elusive. The most dramatic of these is the rebirth narrative that relies on the phoenix metaphor—from ashes comes life anew. Tabachnick, who writes about graphic narratives and makes use of William Howarth's delineation of autobiographical types, suggests one form of the autobiography is "the autobiography of discovery" (102). Autobiographies of discovery are in part an exploration of different aspects of the self and different beliefs held by the self. According to Tabachnick, "only after enormous travail does the authentic belief (the one most suitable for the situation of the autobiographer) emerge, along with an understanding of the self" (102). He suggests that *Epileptic* is a prime example of this category. The quest narrative and the discovery narrative are closely related but not identical. I suggest that both *Epileptic* and *The Spiral Cage* are ultimately quest/discovery narratives that work in different ways. For one, the chaos (and fear) in *The Spiral Cage* is limited and presented in small "chunks," but in *Epileptic* it spills from page to page.

Tabachnick suggests that this discovery process can be delineated through three *moves* by David B. The first is that David discovers his true self through the coping mechanisms of drawing battles and by withdrawing into himself—by "covering himself in psychological armor" (107). His second coping mechanism that moves his quest forward is his attempts to take part in and take seriously the cures of quacks (108) that his parents look to for healing Jean-Christophe' epilepsy. These ultimately fail and leave David discouraged and cynical, but still, they represent a quest, a search. The third is a kind of religious conversion—first he identifies with Jews because of their history of suffering, and finally we see "David's conversion to a secular religion of selflessness" (108) in the epilogue. Tabachnick claims that each of these three ways of coping are necessary for the facilitation of David's discovery of self (108).

It should be pointed out that David does not portray these aspects of quest as clear-cut and direct. For example, when he withdraws into himself, he admits that his armor "protects [him] but isolates [him] as well. It sticks to my skin" (167). "I keep it all to myself" (167). Earlier he lets the reader know that "my armor is becoming increasingly impregnable" (151). In fact, he keeps so much to himself that it is nearly his undoing—his struggles in the midst of the overwhelming chaos not only surround, but nearly engulf him.

Identity formation is complicated by having a brother with such a serious illness. Throughout *Epileptic* the reader meets, and meets again and again, the many selves of David in relationship to his brother. David's feelings about his brother swing from wanting to kill Jean-Christophe, to feeling protective of him. When David feels protective or responsible he wants the family to be in solidarity with Jean-Christophe ("We owe my brother this solidarity"). But as quick as David is to come to Jean-Christophe's defense, he is more often furious with him. In fact, one page later (228) we view a scene that is repeated in a similar form throughout the book. It shows the two brothers fighting with each other and David telling Jean-Christophe he is "lame" (229). We also see multiple scenes in which David "abuses" Jean-Christophe either through physical attacks and/or cruelly by making fun of him. In one especially harsh and memorable scene Beauchard has wrestled Jean-Christophe to the floor and states: "I'm Genghis Kahn and I'm gonna pee in your mouth" (176). In the next panel we see Jean-Christophe's mouth open and David reporting to the reader, perhaps in disgust and disappointment that "he doesn't even try to fight me off (176). For David, this leads to massive confusion about who he is and what he believes. In one early scene David realizes that he can cause Jean-Christophe to have a seizure by making him upset: "I realize that I have a terrifying power over my brother. I'll never play that game again" (38). And in the next sentence of the same panel: "I feel as if I've grown up" (38). Not only is this power terrifying for a now eight-year-old David, but presumably so too is the belief that he is grown up.

As a young adult David makes one desperate attempt to sculpt his identity: he changes his first name from Pierre-François Beauchard to David. This occurs approximately halfway through the book. David exults, "I have not been defeated, I have prevailed over the disease that stalked me" (165). Later he claims that his name change "becomes a way of staking out a position . . . I've begun the process of rebuilding myself" (173). Perhaps he is in search of a new destination map.

Just as *The Spiral Cage* addresses the formation of identity in the face of disability, it is also addressed throughout *Epileptic*. In *Epileptic* identity formation and marginalization are infused throughout by the elaborate drawings of threatening beings, battles, and suffering. In fact David lets us know almost immediately that stigma and marginalization are ubiquitous. Early in *Epileptic* the children in the neighborhood ostracize Jean-Christophe for his seizures and decide he is "crazy" after they have seen him have a seizure. One friend justifies the label "crazy" by claiming "he's always trying to grab us by the throat" (35), to which David replies "No, no, he can tell he's about to fall and he's trying to hang on to someone" (35).

Even when Jean-Christophe is older and he attends the school where his father teaches, the other teachers complain that the epilepsy is too disruptive. Once again, Jean-Christophe's parents are forced to change his school. Throughout the book, one of the most troubling aspects of Jean-Christophe's seizures is when they occur in public and people stare. Beauchard states that "[he] despise[s] people like that

. . . these nice, normal people—their gaze is burned into my memory . . . and it's not over yet" (236). In other words, the social aspect as well as the personal is of constant concern.

But just as David addresses marginalization and stigma out in the world, he also addresses its existence in his own family. In one segment he is speaking with his grandmother who claims that when Jean-Christophe "got the slows" (227) it hurt the children's parents' relationship. David asks her what "the slows" means and she tells him that it "means a little stupid" (227). To this David jumps to Jean-Christophe's defense: "He isn't retarded!" (228) and then we see David's thought: "My poor brother, now you're caught between possession and retardation" (227).

Jean-Christophe's marginalization combines with his illness and takes a toll on everyone, not least of which Jean-Christophe himself. As a child he worships and admires Hitler for his power, and near the end of the book we learn that Jean-Christophe the adult reads *Mien Kampf*. David explains that there is nothing "Nazi-ish" (309) about his choice of reading material, it is, however, "an admission of powerlessness" (309). In other words, Jean-Christophe's powerlessness and dis-affection lead him to reach out not only to the unsavory, but to writing that focuses on identifying "the other" (Jews) as the culprit, the reason for all evil. His own marginalization pushes him to marginalize others.

As a young adult, David attends commercial art school but he keeps to him-self. Eventually be befriends a fellow student, Sophie, who introduces David to a young man who it turns out has a mild form of epilepsy. At this point David tells his two friends about his brother's epilepsy. Simply meeting someone with epilepsy is helpful to David: "That does me good . . . life is suddenly warmer," (312) and being able to talk about his own experiences and loneliness teach him that he too "can tell [his] stories. [He] can talk about [his] life. There are people who will listen to [him]" (312). David is literally finding his voice with others, and learning that he can perhaps overcome his "difficulty . . . getting close to people" (312). It is within his power to reduce his own marginalization. I would say that this is where David's coping mechanisms, suggested by Tabachnick, shift from coping to active steps to be himself. His quest or discovery process is being fleshed out. This is one of the few times that we see David finding some peace in his life. But this peace is short lived: he begins to notice that Sophie has become very distant. When she finally speaks to David she announces that "all that stuff about your brother, it's so heavy . . . I dunno what to do with it. We better not see each other any more" (313–314). Although this begins a new spiral of despair for David that includes his flunking out of art school in the final semester, David has learned that his isolation, his impregnable armor, is making him as disabled as Jean-Christophe. As with his name change David is moving ever closer to identifying his life as a kind of quest.

David's search for identity and some inner peace forms the core of the oft-discussed epilogue as it underscores the point of many selves by including a quo-tation by Portuguese poet Fernando Pessoa ("Sit under the sun. Abdicate and be your own king.") Pessoa is well known for his creation and use of heteronyms. These are different personas created by the poet—they are not pseudonyms, but entire personalities with their own biographies and writing styles. Pessoa wrote by many heteronyms. By quoting Pessoa, one can only imagine that Beauchard is minimally "tipping his hat" to his many selves. In an equally striking way Beauchard's drawings of Jean-Christophe's face continually changes as though he is wearing different masks. At times he appears to be a tiger, a bird, and various indistinguishable beings. In addition the epilogue shows Jean-Christophe and David riding horses together in a fantasy realm. They converse and seem to be in true dialogue, at least briefly, and then they talk past one another as if they are caught in two separate but parallel worlds, akin to young children who participate in parallel play (Fig. 7 p. 359). In one panel Jean-Christophe states that he "chose to be sick because . . . I wanted to stay with mother" (359); to this David responds "I never really found you" (359). There is no obvious "connection" but what there does seem to be is honesty. Jean-Christope admits that he didn't really want to be David's big brother and David admits to Jean-Christophe that he "wanted [Jean-Christophe] to fight, to prevail against the disease" (358), so that Jean-Christophe could still be David's big brother. A panel later David confesses, "I've sought brotherly love in every friendship I've ever struck up" (359). Their conversation may be parallel at times and it may be direct at times, but what the reader is offered appears to be honesty and civility on both their sides. For David, it appears that the chaos is abating at least slightly. Although Tabachnick claims that the epilogue is indicative of a "conversion . . . to selflessness" (108), I do not see it as such, but rather the epilogue *points towards* a less chaotic life and more *self* and *other* understanding.

* * *

One requirement for a significant body of literature of illness and disability narratives is that medical care and medical technology have prolonged and even saved lives that once would have ended rapidly, providing little opportunity for reflection. Today, we know that medical care can often improve life and sometimes prolong life almost indefinitely. This is the result of many things, not least of which is advances in modern medical care, public health, and technology.

But this was not always true: "In the old days . . . folk didn't know what illness was. They went to bed and they died. It's only nowadays that we've learned words like liver, lung, stomach, and I don't know what!" (qtd. in Frank 5). For those with severe disabilities, as opposed to illness, institutionalization or simply a family hiding the disabled away in their own home, was all too often the answer. In some cases, the refusal by the medical community and/or the family to provide the medical care necessary to save the life of a child born with a disability was not uncommon. Today in the United States a full 30% or 62 million people have some kind of disability (CDC 9). Arthur Frank, who studies prose illness narratives refers to

Figure 7. From EPILEPTIC by David B., translated by Kim Thompson, copyright © 2005 by L'Association, Paris, France. Used by permission of Pantheon Books, a division of Random House, Inc.

our culture as a "remission society" (8) because so many illnesses are held at bay. "Sooner or later," he suggests, "everyone is a wounded story teller" (Frank xiii). And Couser reminds us that "disability is the one minority group that anyone can join at any time" (178). In fact, nearly two-thirds of the way through *The Spiral Cage* Al Davison lets the reader know that his mother, father, and sister are all now disabled. His mother is in a wheel chair due to a stroke, his father is disabled by multiple heart attacks, and his sister, although she lives independently, struggles with cerebral palsy, epilepsy, and learning disabilities. In addition, it is well documented that stigma and marginalization of those considered "other" is common. In the area of mental illness, it is stigma alone that many claim to be the most intransigent and destructive of societal responses.

What does the graphic narrative bring to our understanding of present-day illness and disability? What does it offer us, a society that struggles to maintain civility? Graphic narratives offer a uniquely modern approach to addressing illness and disability in our complex, postmodern world. They call on both our verbal and visual skills to present, decipher, and consider the many facets of illness and disability. Couser suggests that visuals are likely to increase stereotypes and thus, stigma. This could be true, but I would argue that visual images bring about a truer and more immediate emotional reaction than prose alone. Prose can neutralize emotional response. Recall the Oklahoma bombing of the Murrah Federal building in 1995. The image that many recall to this day is that of Captain Chris Fields holding the lifeless body of one-year-old Baylee Almon. This one photograph captured, and is still able to capture, the violence, the death, and the toll of this incredible act of terrorism not only against one city, but an entire nation.

The drawings of Davison the adult, especially those of his naked body, can be, like the photograph of Baylee Alom, discomforting yet riveting. In fact I would argue that the graphic narrative, with its visual/verbal grammar, can further the diminishment of stigma and marginalization by their very use of images. According to Whitlock, the power of images to "relay affect and invoke a moral and ethical responsiveness in the viewer regarding the suffering of others" (965) is what fuels comics. In our image-based world they can also articulate the shifting selves with particular poignancy while they show and tell the social impact of being marginalized and stigmatized. Dony and Linthout make the argument that graphic narratives are especially advantageous over other media in representing the "unrepresentable" (181). *Epileptic* succeeds in part because it shows the unrepresentable, and *The Spiral Cage* because it addresses the often unaddressed.

Philosophical anthropologist Martin Buber said that "a soul is never sick alone." Both *Epileptic* and *The Spiral Cage* work to underscore Buber's words. Those perceived as ill or disabled or both, exist in a social context that not only treats them with ambivalence, but also marginalizes them. Illness and disability are societal concerns: they affect all of us. As we face more and more disability due to improved medical care, we will also benefit from medical care that gives us longer and higher quality lives. But at some point, many of us will be disabled, ill or both. At the least, each of us will become more and more fragile. As a civilized society, it is imperative that we work to care for one another. It has been said that the measure of a society is how it treats its weakest members. In some small measure the graphic narrative may be able to facilitate more civilized responses to those who are ill or disabled. As we watch Jean-Christophe seeking solace in *Mein Kampf*, we are reminded of the costs of exclusion, marginalization, and stigma.

NOTES

1. The gutter in comic books/ graphic novels refers to the space between panels. It is where, according to Scott McCloud, much of the "magic and mystery that are at the very heart of comics" (66) takes place. It is "where readers must intuit and define the relationships between different (elements of) images" (Goggin and Hassler-Forest 1-2). Gutter is also the "cultural ghetto" (Goggin and Hassler-Forest 1) in which comics have long existed.

2. Disability is related to but distinct from illness—they are "different conceptual entities" (Couser 177). In fact, many contend that it was not until the 1980s that disability was defined in anything other than medical terms (Squier 2). I am not attempting to blur the lines between them, but to suggest that in many respects the lines are already blurred. Couser suggests that illness can be temporary and addressed by treatment and sometimes cured whereas most disability is permanent and moderated by rehabilitation. In addition, he reminds us that *most* illnesses today are *not* stigmatic, but disability *is* usually stigmatic because those with a disability are often seen as "not self-sufficient" (177). Although these differences exist, Illness can cause disability and disability can cause illness. In the field of disability studies a disability is usually defined as the limitation or handicap that is produced when society does not accommodate an impairment. For example the failure to have wheelchair accessible buses makes anyone in a wheelchair and in need of taking a bus, disabled. An impairment, on the other hand, is usually considered to be an individual's limitation due to a medical problem.

3. Graphic narratives are also referred to as pathographies, among other names. Some believe that the true term is "comic" and that these other terms are to help to make the comic more acceptable in academic circles. I use the term "graphic narrative" because the word "narrative" does not distinguish between fiction and nonfiction, whereas the term "graphic novel' suggests fiction.

4. The graphic narrative has a long history of being considered everything from disgraceful (Versacci 7) to dangerous,v to simply childish (Squier). In 1948 *Time* magazine published "Puddles of Blood," which reported that the violence in comics made them dangerous. Part of the argument was that the increase in juvenile delinquency could be traced to the reading of comic books. The closing words of the article were "Comic books not only inspire evil but suggest a form for the evil to take" (qtd. in Hajdu 97). One of the primary leaders of this anti-comics crusade was a psychiatrist with impressive credentials: Dr. Fredric Wertham. While running a clinic in Harlem he started to do research on the impact of comics on children. Wertham and his colleagues concluded that juvenile delinquency was directly related to comic books. Wertham claimed that ". . . Hitler was a beginner compared to the comic book industry" (qtd. in Hajdu 6). Wertham's "research" and the outcry of others eventually led to Congressional hearings on the evil of comic books. The comics

industry nearly ended. Today most people probably do not consider comics dangerous or poisonous, but many still hold tight to the belief that comics are puerile at best. As Squier points out, "it's considered *normal* in this society for children to combine words and pictures, so long as they *grow out of it* (qtd. In Squier 1).

5. Spina bifida is considered a severe birth defect of the spinal column. The exact cause is still unknown but it includes genetic and environmental factors. Most people with spina bifida confront paralysis, and often hydrocephalus (fluid build-up on the brain) and incontinence. As recently as the 1940s and 1950s, the *mortality* rate was 89% (McLone, 1989). Today that figure is reversed—the vast majority of people born with spina bifida live to adulthoodviii. We are now hearing their voices. Davison's is one of them.

6. Infants with spina bifida usually undergo major surgery within 24 hours of their birth and then, multiple surgeries are usually required throughout childhood and even into adulthood. Al Davison also underwent multiple surgeries.

7. This what McCloud refers to as the reader's work of "observing the parts but perceiving the whole" (63).

8. Spina bifida has an involved history of treatment philosophies. It has ranged from non-treatment to the first successful surgical treatment recorded in 1892 by Bayer. However, even Bayer concluded that surgery should be performed only on those individuals with mild to no hydrocephalus, with and uncomplicated sac, and who are not paralyzed. This was the first selection criteria for the treatment of spina bifida (Shurtleff 1986). Selection criteria were used until the landmark court case of Baby Jane Doe (Stevenson, Araigno, Kutlener, Ernle, and Young). A decision was made to withhold life-saving medical treatment that led to a prolonged legal battle and an eventual addendum o the Child Abuse Protection Bill which specifies the withholding of medically indicated treatment to be illegal.

9. Unlike the several pages of *The Spiral Cage* in which Davison "contains" the darkness by having it appear on one or two pages and within panels, in *Epileptic* the darkness is not contained at all, but spills across pages. This likely reflects the chaos of David's life and the apparent lack of chaos of Davison's.

WORKS CITED

Arnold, Andrew D. "Metaphorically Speaking." *Time Magazine*: n. pag. 1 Jan. 2005. Web.12 Mar. 2011.

Atlas, James. "Confessing for Voyeurs; The age of The Literary Memoir is Now." www.ny-times.com/1996/05/12/magazine/confessing-for-voyeurs-the-age-of-the-literary-memoir-is-now.html?pagewanted=2 12 May, 1996. Web. 22 Jan. 2011.

B. David. *Epileptic*. New York: Pantheon Books, 2005. Print.

Buber, Martin. *Pointing the Way: Collected Essays*. Trans. Maurice. 1957 New York: Harper and Brothers, 1957. (111). Web. 20 Dec. 2010.

CDC: Disability information: www.cdc.gov/nchs/data/misc/disability2001-2005.pdf.

Chute, Hillary. "Our Cancer Year, and: Janet and Me: An Illustrated Story of Love and Loss and: Cancer Vixen: A True Story, and: Mom's Cancer, and: Blue Pills: A Positive Love Story, and: *Epileptic*, and Black Hole." *Literature and Medicine,* vol. 26, no. 2 (Fall 2007): 413–429. Print.

Couser, G. Thomas. *Recovering Bodies: Illness, Disability and Life Writing*. Madison, Wisconsin: U. of Wisconsin P. 1997: Print.

Davison, Al. *The Spiral Cage: An Autobiography*. Astral Gypsy Press: Los Angeles: 2003. Print.

Fiedler, Leslie A. "The Tyranny of the Normal." *The Hastings Center Report*, vol. 14, no. 2: 1984: 40–42. Web. 13 Apr. 2011.

Frank, Arthur. *The Wounded Storyteller: Body, Illness, and Ethics*. U. of Chicago P. 1995.

Gilmore, Leigh. *The Limits of Autobiography: Trauma and Testimony*. Ithaca, New York: Cornell U.P., 2001. Print.

Goggin, Joyce and Dan Hassler-Forest (Eds.). *The Rise and Reason of Comics and Graphic Literature: Critical Essays on the Form*. Jefferson, N.C.: McFarland & Co., Inc. Publishers, 2010. Print.

Hajdu, David. *The Ten-Cent Plague: The Great Comic-Book Scare and How It Changed America*. New York: Farrar, Straus and Giroux, 2008. Print.

Hunsaker-Hawkins, Anne. *Reconstructing Illness: Studies in Pathography*, 2nd. Ed. West Lafayette, Indiana: Purdue U. P. 1999. Print.

Huyssen, Andreas. "Of Mice and Mimesis: Reading Spiegelman with Adorno." *New German Critique*, 81, (Autumn, 2000): 65–82. Print.

Leonard, C. O. and J. M. Freeman. "Spina Bifida: A New Disease." *Pediatrics* 68 (1981): 136–137. Print.

McLone, D. G. "Spina Bifida Today: Problems Adults Face." *Seminars in Neurology*, 9 (1989): 169–176. Print.

Moore, Alan. Introduction. *The Spiral Cage*. By Davison. Los Angeles: Astral Gypsy Press, 2003. Print.

Round, Julia. "'Be vewy, vewy quiet. We're hunting wipers': A Barthesian Analysis of the Construction of Fact and Fiction in Alan Moore and Eddie Campbell's *From Hell*." Joyce Goggin and Dan Hassler-Forest, eds. *The Rise and Reason off Comics and Graphic Literature: Critical Essays on the Form*. North Carolina: McFarland and Co., 2010. 188–201. Print.

Scott, Catherine S. "Time Out of Joint: The Narcotic Effect of Prolepsis in Christopher Reeve's Still Me." *Biography*, 29, no. 2, (Spring 2006): 307–328. Print.

Shelley, Mary W. *Frankenstein: Or the Modern Prometheus*. Boston: Jordan & More Press., 1992. Google Books. Web. 14 Feb. 2011. books.google.com/books?id=QKg-VAAAAYAAJ&printsec=frontcover&dq=Frankenstein++1922&hl=en&ei=UV3qT-bqHLdGtgQfxsPHXCQ&sa=X&oi=book_result&ct=result&resnum=1&ved=0CCsQ6AEwAA#v=onepage&q&f=false.

Shurtleff, D.B. and K. Dunne (Eds.). "Adults and Adolescents with Meningomyelocele." *Myelodysplasias and exstrophies: Significance, prevention, and treatment*. New York Grune & Stratton, 1986. 89–115. Print.

Smith, Sidonie and Julia Watson. *Reading Autobiography: A Guide for Interpreting Life Narratives*, 2nd ed. Minneapolis: U. of Minnesota P., 2010. Print.

Spiegelman, Art. *Maus I: A Survivor's Tale; My Father Bleeds History*. New York: Pantheon, 1986. Print.

———. *Maus II: A Survivor's Tale; And Here My Troubles Began*. New York: Pantheon, 1991. Print.

Squier, Susan M. "So long as they grow out of it: Comics, the Discourse of Developmental Normalcy, and Disability." *Journal of Medical Humanities* (2008): 71–88. Print.

Stevenson, D. K. et al. "The Baby Doe Rule." *Journal of the American Medical Association* 255 (1986): 1909–1912. Print.

Tabachnick, Stephen E. "Autobiography s Discovery in *Epileptic.*" *Graphic Subjects: Critical Essay on Autobiography and Graphic Novels.* Michael A. Chaney, Ed. Madison Wisconsin: U. of Wisconsin P. 2011. 101–116. Print.

Versaci, Rocco. *This Book Contains Graphic Language: Comics as Literature.* New York: Continuum International Publishing Group, Inc., 2007. Print.

Whitlock, Gillian. *Autographics: The Seeing "I" of the Comics.* Modern Fiction Studies 2, no. 4, (Winter 2006): 965–979. Print.

CHAPTER FIVE

A Teacher Educator's Re-imagining: Finding Places and Making Spaces for Transformative Civility in Schools

Carol M. Pate

When the Center for Disease Control (CDC) identifies youth violence as a significant public health and school safety issue (2010), clearly civility is nearing a holy grail status of attainment for far too many of our nation's schools. Over 5.5% of high school adolescents and young adults in our nation's schools leave school early for fear of being bullied (CDC, 2010), and over 15 crimes per thousand students were reported in over 62% of public schools (Robers, S., Zhang, J., and Truman, J., 2010). In schools where 75% of students receive free or reduced cost lunch, the reporting of discipline problems (bullying, student racial/ethnic and gender identity tensions/sexual harassment) compared to schools where only 25% or fewer students receive free or reduced meals is statistically significant (Robers, S., Zhang, J., & Truman, J., 2010). Private schools (includes religiously-affiliated schools) are also not immune from problems; 50% of students and teachers report the existence of gangs and gang-related activity (Robers, S., Zhang, J., & Truman, J., 2010). A full 70% of all reported students identified schools as the primary site where incidences of bullying occurred (Robers, S., Zhang, J., & Truman, J., 2010).

There is no shortage of blame, nor "blameworthy candidates" (Egan, 1997, locations 35–36; Kindle Edition) for this situation. The candidates (families, social and political institutions, modern culture with new social media availability) fling blame in and around the situation, looking at many places and spaces outside of their worlds to find someone or something on which to lay the wreath of shame.

In defense of the candidates, a myriad of school and community-based programs funded by public and private dollars are spent to assist in solving this seemingly intractable issue. Billions of dollars has supported significant print, digital and social media public education resources, and significant dollars expended by nationally-known television/movie; political, or other corporations/organizations/individuals to raise awareness and promote specific responses. For example, in response to the 1999 Columbine High School shooting, the Surgeon General developed a report highlighting the latest scientific/evidenced-based research and identifiers of model and promising programs for nationwide dissemination and use (Youth Violence: A Report of the Surgeon General, 2001). What is deeply troubling however is that while billions of dollars are being spent to reduce violence/uncivil behaviors and actions among our young people in school settings, over the past five years there has been little to no change in the statistics (CDC, 2010; Robers, S., Zhang, J., and Truman, J., 2010).

Much of the difficulty lies in the sheer complexity of the situation. Schools are places and spaces of social/cultural action and interaction with all the attendant issues of power differentials; competition for resources; needs for status and identity, and individual/cultural needs to be acknowledged and accepted (Burgess & Burgess, 2003). Centered in communities of local, state and national histories of social/cultural interactions, schools as microcosms of society is more than just a slogan, it is patently clear that today's schools have all the elements that give rise to social conflicts. With schooling a mandatory requirement for all young persons (to age 16 in most states); one might consider the statistics cited above moderate in comparison to what television/media hypes as reality. Nevertheless, the issue of incivility in schools calls for more of what Egan (1997) terms a "polysemous" (locations 64–74, Kindle edition) understanding, one that comes from multiple perspectives, places and spaces of social and cultural interactions within a school setting. If we are going to have any positive impact on civility as it is experienced, perhaps a more polysemous understanding would assist in re-imagining a future where our young people would indeed experience something akin to transformative civility. Such an experience could then recapitulate a civility that would be more available for solving some of the larger society's concerns and issues as they begin their lives as young adult citizens. My goal in this chapter is first to offer a preliminary polysemous understanding of incivility through the lens of the Beyond Intractability Knowledge Base Project of the University of Colorado, co-directed and edited by Guy and Heidi Burgess (2003). These authors have compiled what might be arguably the most comprehensive information available to assist society to come to an appreciative understanding of the multiple components, perspectives and issues surrounding social conflict. While the extensive library of documents refers primarily to conflicts experienced at state/national/international levels, parallels to the microcosm of schools will be drawn. The parallels to schools will utilize Egan's (1997) conception of how incompatibilities within the educational system's three primary philosophical underpinnings further complicate and exacerbate conflicts. Thus, proposed resolutions to the increase of violence in one of the most critical microcosms of our society are inadequate. From a weaving of Burgess & Burgess's (2003) social conflict knowledge base with a portrait of schools as being held hostage by conflicts, this chapter will conclude with some thoughts on what might be called transformative civility. It is a beginning conversation, one this author hopes will continue through her work and collaborative endeavors.

CIVILITY THROUGH THE LENS OF SOCIAL CONFLICT

When civility is defined as "politeness" towards others one may disagree with this definition. Society certainly has seen less and less of it in public places of discourse, including town hall meetings and now, social media such as the Internet (Deever, 2010). However, according to Neblo (2010, in Deever, 2010), politeness is not the only component. "Civil discourse is not the same as polite, unemotional discourse. Democracies sometimes need passionate protest, and civil disobedience can actually be a duty in extreme cases (Neblo, 2010, p. 10, in Deever, 2010). Burgess and Burgess (1997, 2003) advance a definition that places civility in the center of social conflict, a place where individuals on multiple sides of an issue can increase the constructiveness of the debate, quarrel, or disagreement through the use of strategies primarily designed to de-personalize the conflict. In short, with our increasing global, multicultural, multi-interest society, conflict is inevitable. While 21st century society blames a culture of narcissism for the increase in incivility, social media advances that have erased social boundaries that heretofore were preserved have upped the complexity of the situation (Deever, 2010). Therefore, the knowledge and skills gained through understanding a more polysemous nature of social conflict is critical to begin a re-imagining of the possibility of transformative civility.

Social conflict arises from several major issues, only a few of which can be illuminated here to draw a preliminary but focal sketch. Major areas of conflict include distributional (Burgess, H., 2004), rich-poor (Barbanti, Jr., O., 2003), social status (Maiese, M., 2004), identity (Kriesberg, K., 2003), unmet needs (Maiese, M., 2003) ; and moral, justice or rights (Maiese, M., 2003) issues. Burgess (2003) writes that distributional issues are mainly issues of resources; where disagreements over who gets what and how much is received are highlighted. She further reveals that the "item to be distributed is usually tangible—money, land, better houses, better schools, or better jobs, for example. But the item to be distributed can be intangible as well. For example, siblings competing for a parent's love could be considered a distributional conflict (Burgess, H., 2003). If there is not enough to either satisfy everyone, or there is not enough to distribute equitably to all who may need or want it, then the issue can become a win-lose conflict (Burgess, H., 2003). The rich-poor issue concerns broadly the economic status of a community, state or nation (Barbanti, Jr., O., 2003), where individuals can live in absolute (clearly defined standards/levels of measurement) poverty conditions or relative poverty conditions (conditions that change over time and are related to lifestyle issues). Social status is understood to be the degree to which society attaches a certain prestige or position level depending on one's role(s), income,, education, or other factors (Maiese, M., 2004). Identity issues concern the Us versus Them schema, where culture, religion, ethnicity, gender, sexual orientation to name a few, become categories that divide issues (Kriesberg, K., 2003). Unmet needs include the biological (food and water) and the social (human bonding) (Maiese, M., 2003). Issues of morals (religious, cultural beliefs), justice (norms or entitlements leading to decent treatment) or rights (making a claim) contribute highly to the existence of conflicts (Maiese, M., 2003).

The majority of the issues noted above are identified as sitting near the intractability side of the conflict continuum (Burgess, G., and Burgess, H., 2003). Intractability is a way of understanding conflicts that do "substantial harm, yet the parties seem unable to extricate themselves—either alone or with outside help. This is because the perceived costs of getting out are still seen as higher than the costs of staying in (Kriesberg, 2003) These conflicts resist resolution due to an "intricate set of historical, religious, cultural, political, and economic issues (Maiese, M., 2003, paragraph 2) that have been in existence for a long period of time. It can be said that the decreasing level of civil behaviors are due to the extent that societal conflicts have become more intractable. Certainly it is evident that our society has an increasing multicultural population, increasing pockets of poverty, a decrease in social boundaries due to increased access to social media, a rise in fundamentalism in religious/moral values, and/or a rise in a polarization of political views. To what extent these factors contribute to a more intractable level of conflict creating greater levels of uncivil behavior in schools at this point in time has not been comprehensively understood.

Civility in Schools

In addition to the family and church, 19th and 20th century schools were thought to be the primary place for young citizens to be inculcated into the proper forms of behaviors/moral reasoning/virtuous actions. Students attending private or boarding schools received more of the ethical/moral reasoning curriculum (as well as a more intellectual science/liberal arts curriculum) supported by reading of philosophers such as Plato or Kant. This was compared to young children and adolescents attending public schools who were given McGuffey Readers and the Bible to inculcate proper behaviors and manners, as well as the basics of reading, writing and arithmetic. Given that there was general agreement over the school's right, ability and accountability in the teaching of civil values, most schools were judged to serve their purpose in society. Fast forward to the 21st century, and what has changed?

Egan's (1997) premise of why schools are dysfunctional is that 19th century schools have combined three primary educational ideologies/philosophies, that when revealed for their aims and goals, are mutually incompatible. The first idea espoused by Plato privileged specific forms of knowledge to bring about a realistic and rational view of the world. The specific forms of knowledge included the sciences, mathematics, and philosophy; anything that would support "direct knowledge of the real, the true, the good and the beautiful" (Egan, 1997, locations 261–70). Plato believed it is knowledge and the acquisition of it that drives human development. The intellectual cultivation aim is to ensure that students acquire knowledge of the world that is above the everyday concerns of society; to "connect children to this great cultural conversation" (Egan, 1997, Locations 216–225). This great cultural conversation is the content of the liberal arts and sciences (including mathematics), highly valued as a greater contribution to society than auto mechanics (Egan, 1997).

The second worldview was that schools were to serve as the primary socializing agency for the young as they were being readied to enter into the cultural norms of adult society. A curriculum based in this philosophy included the vocational as well as practical arts, and the three "R's" of reading, writing and arithmetic. Schools served as primary hegemonic influences to ensure its future citizens would be ready to participate in the workforce and perpetuate the knowledge, skills and values deemed appropriate by the dominant culture. First, proponents of the socialization ideology believed that children were to be socialized according to the knowledge, skills and dispositions held by the adults in the surrounding communities. Their socialization aim holds that schools are to be accountable to society for students who "graduate with an understanding of their society and of their place and possibilities within it, that they have the skills required for it perpetuation, and they hold its values and commitments" (Egan, 1997, Locations 160–69, Kindle Edition). Thus, the socialization aim is to create citizens that untrouble the current systems in society.

The third philosophy of education was developed by Rousseau who had significant misgivings about Plato's idea of preparing the young to participate in the elite sciences (Egan, 1997). In *EMILE*, Rousseau provided a portrait of what education would look like if we focused our attention on the internal development process and its interaction with the outside world. His idea was that only when society focuses on the more humane process of education would we be sure that children and young adults could develop to their full potential (Egan, 1997). Finally, Rousseau's ideology highlighted the need and value for individualizing education that was focused on the developing nature of the child. (Egan, 1997). Rousseau believed that it is development that drives the acquisition of knowledge and skills more suited to the specific nature of children and young adults (Egan, 1997).

Today, one finds the majority of schools supporting a curriculum that is a combination of Plato's grand cultural conversations, Rousseau's developmentally appropriate curriculum and American society's vocationally focused training in an attempt to fulfill all three aims (Egan, 1997). Another way to consider the three ideologies is knowledge centered vs. individual development-centered vs. society-centered. Throughout the 20th and the beginning of the 21st century, the structural configuration, curriculum focus and public and private resources given to educate a growing diverse population of students depended greatly on which influence gained prominence; either the current scientific research in educational practices, biological/psychological/social understandings of development or the political climate.

The incompatibilities uncovered in the philosophical foundations of American schooling seem to also have exacerbated and complicated any efforts to reduce uncivil behavior in the schools. A primarily knowledge-centered education for civility would be a Plato-like approach of supporting moral reasoning skills in young children and adolescents. This may or may not be essential to civility, as a moral person might express his/her morals/values in an uncivil-like manner. The individual development-centered approach that honors something within each individual might choose character education as a way to influence desirable qualities or traits. However, character education may not view the need to act for the common, as opposed to the individual, good. The society-centered approach might choose to use social skills education as a way to teach specific behaviors to maximize social reinforcement. However, this misses an essential ingredient in civility, the sense of individual participation and choice in an interaction with others. The incompatibility of these civility aims exacerbates the difficulties to adequately respond to emerging and increasing school-based conflicts. It is no wonder that the billions of dollars spent on various youth violence prevention programs has had spotty success.

There is, I propose, an additional compelling influence on all children and adolescents in today's society that has added fuel to the conflict fire. The compelling influence I contend is the proliferation of individual digital video and communication technology devices that allow anonymous interactions. The 1970's brought video games into American households, and with improved graphics and the ability to interact over the Internet with other players across the globe, the number of young people engaging in simulated-violence has increased greatly (Farrales, 2001). Farrales (2001) reviewed research regarding the correlation between the number of hours of watching television and playing violence-oriented video games and found an increase in aggressive verbal behaviors as well as physical play among all younger age (elementary school-aged) groups. Females were most affected, as they had fewer exposures to violent activities and thus were more negatively influenced. College students had increased heart rates and expressed increased hostility during tests (Farrales, 2001).

More recently, the addition of digital communication devices such as mobile phones, iPods, PDA's (personal device assistants); and IPads (Hertz, David-Ferdon, 2008) combined with widespread permissibility of children and adolescents to access and engage with their peers and others through these digital devices has increased exponentially the network of "others" with whom to converse and engage. The Center for Disease Control (CDC) coined the term "electronic aggression" to refer to all types of violence that occur electronically (Hertz, David-Ferdon, 2008). They define electronic aggression as "Any type of harassment or bullying (teasing, telling lies, making fun of someone, making rude or mean comments, spreading rumors, or making threatening or aggressive comments) that occurs through email, a chat room, instant messaging, a website (including blogs), or text messaging" (p. 3). Parents, teachers, and the public understand electronic aggression by the terms popular press terms including cyberbullying, Internet-harassment or Internet-bullying (Hertz, David-Ferdon, 2008). CDC research indicates that unfortunately, this is the fastest growing and most intractable form of violence by our children and young people to their peers (Hertz, David-Ferdon, 2008) with a range of 9–35% of children and youth ages 10–17 reported being a victim of electronic aggression (Hertz, David-Ferdon, 2008). Electronic aggression is associated with emotional distress and conduct problems at school, much like traditional forms of youth violence (Hertz, David-Ferdon, 2008).

What is most revealing about the 2008 CDC brief, is that out of eight recommendations to help decrease electronic aggressive behaviors, creating a positive school climate was number seven (Hertz, David-Ferdon, 2008). Recommendations one through six involved the review and development of electronic aggression prevention policies. While within the recommendations there were statements of the importance of a positive school environment, it was in the context of policy. Included were policy recommendations for the review and use of specific bullying prevention programs (Hertz, David-Ferdon, 2008).

I would submit that electronic aggression, combined with more traditional forms of bullying and other school violence incidents appears now to meet the definition of an intractable conflict as defined earlier in this chapter. An interwoven set of historical, cultural, political, and economic issues (Maiese, M., 2003) have to some degree been identified here. First, there is a history of dysfunctional schooling due to the combination of three primary incompatible educational aims. These aims have been supported by various economic and political climates, policies and procedures. In addition, within the schools there has been a significant increase in school violence in both traditional forms and increasingly electronic aggressive forms. The high permissibility and significant economic access to various digital devices, along with more open access to handguns especially in urban communities, has significantly changed the landscape of schooling.

What possible path could this change in the schooling landscape create that would not be a recapitulation of the solutions/recommendations given by the various public health, educational theorists and/or other policy experts? One thought is to look more thoroughly into social structural change theories, ones that do not identify quick support resolutions that do more to cover up or divert attention from the more deeply embedded intricate threads of the situation. John Lederach (2003) began using the term conflict transformation as compared to conflict resolution to highlight a considerably different level of commitment and work necessary to support a positive outcome for these more intractable conflicts. The term arose out of the Anabaptist-Mennonite religious framework that emphasizes peace as embedded in justice, the building of right relationships and social structures through a radical respect for human rights and non-violence as way of life (Lederach, 2003). Conflict transformation work uses extensive writing and research that both acknowledges conflict as normal in human relations and that conflict can also be an engine for change (Lederach, 2003). The process of transformation considerably changes the way we relate to ourselves, to one another and even to larger groups.

Lederer (2003) sees conflict transformation as a lens that views non-violent interactions as centered and rooted in quality relationships. Included are face-to-face interactions and the ways in which our social, political, economic, and cultural relationships are structured. In today's world, the addition of virtual places and spaces from which digital interactions occur also count. In this sense, conflict transformation is simultaneously dynamic, adaptive, and changing. It is defined by intentional efforts to address the natural rise of human conflict through approaches that address issues and increase understanding, equality, care and respect in relationships (Lederach, 2003). Conflict transformational processes are about way of looking and seeing from which to make sense of social conflict. By drawing attention to certain aspects, the overall meaning of the conflict comes into sharper focus (Lederach, 2003).

An understanding of Lederach's (2003) writings and research regarding intractable conflicts provides a hopeful horizon to finding places and making spaces for transformational civility in schools. His research suggests the need to develop capacities to engage in change processes at the interpersonal, inter-group, and social-structural levels (Lederach, 2003). One set of capacities would thus point toward teachers and other staff members who interact with students on a daily basis. At the same time, efforts are needed to see, pursue, and create change organizing social structures, beginning with the classroom, school and district. This requires capacity to understand and sustain dialogue as a fundamental means of constructive change (Lederach, 2003).

If we were to re-imagine schools as places of transformational civility with dialogue as the key component to creating, maintaining and evaluating the quality relationships, William Ury's, *The Third Side: Why We Fight and How We Can Stop* (2000) might be a place to begin. In his book, Ury summarizes the foundations of conflict and its possible transformation through the use of third side roles (2000). Conflict is assumed to be a natural part of our human lives; violence is not (Ury, 2000). A Third side takes the larger community perspective in supporting a transformation from conflict to resolution. Third side roles are specific ways individuals support relationships in an attempt to prevent, resolve or contain conflicts (Ury, 2000).

Schools as places of complex social-structural relationships where more formalized learning is placed could benefit from this perspective. The civility aim would be to create and sustain quality and just relationships throughout the school and community by identifying individuals to assist in the prevention, resolving and where necessary, containing, social conflicts. Viable roles for community members as well as school personnel would be the norm. The first two levels of transformation contain the roles dedicated to prevent and support sustainable resolutions to prevent conflicts from escalating into violence. Prevention roles include providers, teachers and bridge-builders. The provider (usually the principal) ensures the safety and other basic needs of his/her school personnel and students. The teacher (all teachers) would utilize specific strategies to create and maintain positive supportive relationships ensuring that care and boundaries of behaviors were a regular part of his/her classroom experience where respect and connectiveness are apparent. This role could arguably be one of the most important roles of a teacher as s/he would be the model of respectful and supportive conversation and dialogue. Knowledge and experience with practices such as conversation circles; restorative practices/justice and other evidenced-based strategies inclusive of all learners would be imperative. The bridge-builder would identify and anticipate the possibility of relationships in conflict across natural divides outside the classroom setting. One example would be to identify potential conflicts that would occur across grade levels, and developing systems to reduce the possibility of conflicts.

Resolving roles would include a mediator, arbiter, equalizer and healer. These roles are designed to provide supports for individuals involved in a particular conflict, to ensure that justice was part of the equation and to support dialogue and other measures to heal any emotional wounds that might result from conflicts. These roles could definitely involve community members depending on past experience and expertise. Restorative justice strategies utilize individuals to support the resolution of conflicts that attempts to restore a positive relationship and prevent further conflicts.

Finally, containing roles include witness, referee and peacekeepers. Witnesses observe the school from many vantage points; they are alert and report escalation of behaviors likely to result in conflicts. Referees provide and monitor boundaries to behaviors and assist in the ending of behaviors if the lines have been crossed or breached. Finally, peacekeepers are the last resort in a situation when it gets significantly out of the boundaries of acceptableness and concern for the physical safety of individuals is observed. Containing roles also would include monitoring the use of digital devices in an effort to reduce the anonymity of interactions. Many local, state and national policies serve in some measure as containing roles.

In conclusion, the possibility for all schools to find places and make spaces for a conflict transformational approach to civility exists. The conflict transformational approach begins right where the school is, using the existing conflicts as an engine to seek and find the areas of needed prevention, resolving and containing conflicts. Policies and procedures are necessary but abstract boundaries for primarily containment concerns, the Zero-tolerance policies for bullying is one striking example. Rather than more policies, what is needed in schools is identification and support for knowledge and competences of behaviors that develop, support and maintain positive relationships and engaged learning. Knowledgeable and experienced individuals, organizations and agencies in the community would be critical and valuable partners of the process.

Schools continue to be a crucial and valued polysemous social-structural relationship which society needs to ensure that its future citizens value relationships and connections to the world as much as needed knowledge and skills for the economics of life. Transformational civility is a re-imagining which acknowledges and honors the complexity of individual and group dynamics in school settings, especially those residing in communities where histories of oppression and disconnection to the larger society live. The proliferation of digital devices has increased the complexity of relatedness even more. Transformational civility accepts conflict as part of the human dynamic while at the same time makes it a mission to support and teach transformative processes utilizing the community to serve needed roles. It does not cover or hide the extensive difficulties that would be experienced in beginning this path. However, if the path were taken, one could foresee school walls being transformed into corridors of safety, care and learning. Its halls would become paths to multiple and diverse engaged relationships where conflict is transformed into resolutions that build rather than tear connections. Classrooms in all communities could become environments for focused intellectual, social and artistic engagements with their peers, teachers and school personnel, community members, and with the Internet, global relationships. The question is does society have the will to assist in this process? The jury is still out.

WORKS CITED

Barbanti, Jr., Olympio (2003). "Development and Conflict." *Beyond Intractability*. Eds. Guy Burgess and Heidi Burgess. Conflict Research Consortium, University of Colorado, Boulder. Posted: August 2004 www.beyondintractability.org/essay/development_conflict_introduction/ Retrieved on May 16, 2011.

Burgess, Heidi. "High-Stakes Distributional Issues." *Beyond Intractability*. Eds. Guy Burgess and Heidi Burgess. Conflict Research Consortium, University of Colorado, Boulder. Posted:January 2004 www.beyondintractability.org/essay/distribution_issues/ Retrieved on May 16, 2011.

Burgess, Heidi and Guy M. Burgess. "What Are Intractable Conflicts?." *Beyond Intractability*. Eds. Guy Burgess and Heidi Burgess. Conflict Research Consortium, University of Colorado, Boulder. Posted: November 2003 www.beyondintractability.org/essay/meaning_intractability/. Retrieved on May 16, 2011.

Center for Disease Control. *Understanding School Violence*. Posted January, 2010 at www.cdc.gov/violenceprevention/pdf/schoolviolence_factsheet-a.pdf. Retrieved on May 16, 2011.

Deever, J. Uncivil Discourse. *Ohio State Alumni Magazine*. September–October, 2010.

DeVoe, J.F., and Bauer, L. (2010). *Student Victimization in U.S. Schools: Results From the 2007 School Crime Supplement to the National Crime Victimization Survey* (NCES

2010–319). U.S. Department of Education, National Center for Education Statistics, Institute of Educational Sciences,Bureau of Justice Statistics, Washington, DC: U.S. Government Printing Office.

Egan, K. (1997) *The Educated Mind: How Cognitive Tools Shape Our Understanding*. University of Chicago Press, Chicago, IL. Kindle Edition Retrieved on May 16, 2011.

Farrales, B. (2003) Violence in Video Games. Retrieved from cseserv.engr.scu.edu/ StudentWebPages/BFarrales/ResearchPaper.htm—Cached on May 16, 2011.

Hertz, M.F., David-Ferdon C. *Electronic Media and Youth Violence: A CDC Issue Brief for Educators and Caregivers*. Atlanta (GA): Centers for Disease Control; 2008. Retrieved from www.cdc.gov/violenceprevention/pdf/EA-brief-a.pdf on April 26, 2011.

Kriesberg, Louis. "Countering Intractability." *Beyond Intractability*. Eds. Guy Burgess and Heidi Burgess. Conflict Research Consortium, University of Colorado, Boulder. Posted: October 2003 www.beyondintractability.org/essay/countering_intractability/>. Retrieved on April 26, 2011.

Lederach, John Paul. "Conflict Transformation." *Beyond Intractability*. Eds. Guy Burgess and Heidi Burgess. Conflict Research Consortium, University of Colorado, Boulder. Posted: October 2003 www.beyondintractability.org/essay/transformation/> Retrieved on May 16, 2011.

Maiese, Michelle. "Justice Conflicts." *Beyond Intractability*. Eds. Guy Burgess and Heidi Burgess. Conflict Research Consortium, University of Colorado, Boulder. Posted: July 2003 www.beyondintractability.org/essay/justice_conflicts/>. Retrieved on April 26, 2011.

Maiese, Michelle. "Causes of Disputes and Conflicts." *Beyond Intractability*. Eds. Guy Burgess and Heidi Burgess. Conflict Research Consortium, University of Colorado, Boulder. Posted: October 2003 www.beyondintractability.org/essay/underlying_causes/>. In Peter Coleman, "Intractable Conflict," in *The Handbook of Conflict Resolution: Theory and Practice*, eds. Morton Deutsch and Peter Coleman, (San Francisco: Jossey-Bass Inc., 2000), 428. Retrieved on May 16, 2011.

Neblo, M. Quotation from interview in Deever, J., Uncivil Discourse. *Ohio State Alumni Magazine*. September–October, 2010., 9.

Robers, S., Zhang, J., and Truman, J. (2010). *Indicators of School Crime and Safety: 2010* (NCES 2011-002/NCJ 230812). National Center for Education Statistics, U.S. Department of Education, and Bureau of Justice Statistics, Office of Justice Programs, U.S. Department of Justice. Washington, DC. Retrieved from nces.ed.gov/ pubs2011/2011002.pdf, on May 16, 2011.

Youth Violence: A Report of the Surgeon General, January 2001. Retrieved from www.surgeongeneral.gov/library/youthviolence/youvioreport.htm on May 16, 2011.

CHAPTER SIX

Towards a Compassionate Conversation: The Art of Spiritual Direction

Carolynne Ervin

Conversation is a part of everyday life; yet there are times when it proves to be challenging to actually "hear" what another is saying. Did you ever notice that when you enter into conversation with some people, that there is a spark of energy ignited? There is an interior recognition that the other person is listening to you, understanding you, and wanting to respond to you. With others, however, there is a blank stare, a disinterested look or a sense of boredom.

In many places in today's world, ordinary conversation is a lost art. Interruptions, distractions, and electronic devices are but a few of the ways that ordinary conversation is diverted or detoured into a brief or rote response or tweet. Even as we watch commercials on television, people are not talking or listening to each other.

A practice has been passed down through many faith traditions[1] which develops listening to another with individual attention. This practice is called spiritual direction.[2] The term "spiritual director" is actually a misnomer because the director does not make decisions for the individual. The person comes seeking deeper conversation in order to arrive at her own clarities and decisions. Today, it is more appropriate to use the term spiritual companion or guide[3] because the task is to walk with the person on her journey.

Spiritual Direction is the art of conversation focused on God's power and activity in our everyday lives. This narrative[4] of lived life experience contains the key elements of a person's faith journey, whether we call it "spiritual" or not. In spiritual direction, there is a concerted effort to really "hear" what the other is saying. In training programs for spiritual direction, some of the skills taught are noticing, evoking, discerning and responding.[5] This essay will discuss each of these skills and how they contribute to greater understanding among people.

These skills are not merely techniques; they are ways of engaging others and eliciting more of the individual's story. It is the effort to discover the "moment" when something stirred within them that shifted their awareness and touched their heart. It is a gift and a challenge to help another person articulate that moment.

What does this deeper kind of conversation look like? Spiritual direction is ordinarily a one-to-one experience where the desire of the directee directs the exploration of how the Holy One permeates life for them. The role of the director is to assist the person telling their story, and to explore the story by opening up areas of energy for further reflection and consideration. It is to listen with attentiveness and non-judgment to what the person wants to share. It is to listen without a personal agenda.

For me, spiritual direction pertains to the heart of a person's relationship with God. I image my heart compassionately paying attention to the directee's heart, both being held in God's compassionate heart. This conversation in spiritual direction opens up when the person's life and experiences come from a perspective of faith. Participating in spiritual direction is a free response to God's invitation to live an authentic life. I do not know what a person holds in her heart until she shares it with me. My attentive listening is what matters as I offer a contemplative and compassionate presence to the directee.

How I respond to the directee varies depending on what the person is sharing. Sometimes I just nod my head; other times I ask questions in order to clarify my understanding of the experience. At other times, I invite the directee to notice more about what is happening in the experience—both within themselves and with God. There is no script or road map for this. Interaction depends on my capacity to listen and then discern with the directee how to respond to the presence of the Holy One.

And so the conversation unfolds as the person shares her story and the director notices what is occurring, evokes more reflection, assists discerning what movements are happening, and responds to both consoling moments and desolating moments with patience and gentleness.

NOTICING

Noticing[6] involves paying attention to the directee and hearing what the directee is saying by looking at the experience, seeing what gestures the directee uses to express herself. Sometimes, it is important to listen without interruption; at such times, a smile, a nod of the head, a brief comment is all that is necessary for the person to know the spiritual director is engaged in her story. At other times noticing involves slowing down the narrative in order to help the directee notice and enter more deeply into the experience.

I recently had a directee who said, "There's so much I need to share with you, I hardly know where to begin." That was my cue to listen without interruption. I waited for the story to unfold before I began to explore her experience.

What was I noticing? I was paying attention to the presence of the Holy One, Jesus or God, as the person understands or approaches the Divine. Sometimes God-language is explicit; at other times, it is not. There is, however, a sense of rightness or congruence within the individual which the director senses. This is a time of searching for the Sacred in everyday life and in ordinary situations.

The purpose of spiritual direction is first to assist the directee to tell her/his story. It does not depend on explicit religious language or metaphors. It has to do with the movement of the person's heart. In spiritual direction, what we have is the narrative of the person's journey. By careful listening, I hold that narrative with reverence and humility knowing that I will receive more knowledge of the journey with each subsequent session. It is like weaving a tapestry. The threads appear and become woven together through intertwining themes and motifs together so that an image or picture evolves. Someone told me that we humans see only what is under the tapestry while God sees the image on the other side. There is no pattern to follow until the voice of the directee indicates the direction in which to proceed.

This does not mean that I am sitting back and doing nothing. I am actively engaged in listening by staying with the experience of the directee and exploring, discerning, and responding to her so that they receive clarity, understanding, and self-knowledge.

EVOKING

As the conversation unfolds, the director often evokes[7] further awareness of the experience by eliciting more thoughts, feelings, images, or sensations. Evoking means asking appropriate questions, such as, "Can you say more about that?" or mirroring back to the individual significant words or phrases. This may lead to further awareness and understanding of the experience. The directee realizes that she is being heard in a new way. Staying with experience and not going off on a tangent is helpful so the person can allow the experience to settle within her. Timing is key. What to ask, when, and how, all reveal the director's resonance with the directee. I am not necessarily seeking information for its own sake, I am trying to bring some awareness into clear focus. Sometimes it is enough to wonder with the directee if there is an image or a metaphor which captures the essence of the story.

DISCERNING

This naturally leads into discerning[8] and exploring how the movements are going towards or away from the Sacred. I use the language of Movement and Countermovement to describe this interior experience.[9] Movement, equivalent to consolation in the classical sense described by Ignatius of Loyola,[10] is felt awareness which draws and attracts me towards the Holy One. Countermovement, on the other hand, equivalent to desolation, is a felt awareness that interrupts the flow of thoughts and feelings and disconnects me from being drawn towards the Holy One. Instead, I am moving away. Often, there is a feeling of being jarred which indicates countermovement.

Discerning means sifting and sorting present interior movements so that I know which ones lead to the Sacred and which ones do not. This is not simplistic; it takes a lifetime to learn the art of discernment and put it into practice in daily life. Articulating struggles with a spiritual director becomes more fruitful when the person gains her own sense of what fits and what does not fit. The directee may be looking at a particular ministry and wonder if it fits for them. Does it fit their call to greater freedom within themselves? Does this choice fit their lifestyle? At times using the image of balance assists the person to identify if there are obstacles which prevent balance or fears that surface when trying to make a decision. The person needs a sense of interior freedom to embrace the choice that most suits her situation and circumstance. Their uniqueness surfaces as they become clear on what matters and what doesn't.

RESPONDING

When struggle surfaces, I need to stay with the person and help her assess what is happening. So, here, I might ask questions of a different sort. For example, I might ask "What was it like when you were in balance?[11] Is there an image for this? What happens to this image when you are "out of balance"? Is there some resistance going on which is interfering with interior freedom? What support does the individual need from me so they can engage this? Is there self-doubt, fear or worry? These are but the tip of the dilemma. Helping an individual sort out these threads often reveals deeper hesitations, difficulties and resistances.

When working with women, in particular, empowering them to have a sense of their own authority is vital. We often hear the expression "in her own voice." Spiritual direction is just that. Giving a woman a chance to tell her story "in her own voice." Naming God[12] in ways that are fitting for her and fostering new images to describe her relationships are all part of the journey.

The director knows the answers lie within the directee. The desire is to elicit this interior wisdom from the directee's personal self- knowledge and awareness. Appealing to the woman's sense of integrity and honesty within herself often reveals a new truth or insight or just a general sense of well being. This flows throughout the body and attests to the authenticity of the person's story as she presents it in the spiritual direction conversation.

The conversation frames the struggle for clarity. It is a labyrinthian path that unfolds as the individual continues to seek her deepest truth and find her interior place of centering. What unfolds through these conversations over time is deeper understanding of the self, others, the world. Further, all of this becomes a way to experience the Sacred in all aspects of life.

Another metaphor is that of a dance.[13] As a spiritual director, I partner with the directee to encourage her natural movement and rhythm. Is today's session a waltz or a tango? Is the conversation fast paced and excited or slow and quiet? *The gift and skill of a spiritual director is to partner no matter the style of dance or the pace.* Each directee brings her unique personality and faith stance to the director. It is the task of the director to adapt her way of being to each person. I find that gentleness is a compassionate art and a skill which needs to be interwoven throughout the conversation.

There is an interior resonance that occurs when there is a fit between director and directee. This is a mutual experience. An intuitive understanding and capacity to reflect back to the directee occur spontaneously. Such intuitive understanding is both intangible in some aspects and tangible in others. This is part of the mystery of God's Spirit as I collaborate with God in this transforming ministry of spiritual direction.

The Mystery of the Divine permeates every session of spiritual direction. The journey to awareness for the directee is revealed gradually and over time. I stay with the process as it unfolds. I do not hurry it. I wait with the directee for the next moment/Movement to reveal itself.

As this understanding and awareness of self, of others, of situations in our world deepens, the directee has greater capacity to receive not just her own story but the stories of others.

As I draw the spiritual direction conversation to a close, I want to gather the fragments of the conversation and provide a way for the directee to appropriate what has just occurred. I might ask simply, "How do you feel now?" or "Has anything shifted since you began sharing today?" Another way of initiating this part of the conversation is to ask, "What are you taking with you that you didn't have when you arrived?"

In a compassionate conversation, the directee leaves with a sense of peace and harmony, for the most part, even though there still may be issues to process. The encounter of spiritual direction offers an alternative to using preplanned remedies for life's difficulties. The on-going practice of discernment deepens when the directee regularly meets with a spiritual director.

It is my hope that this essay has illuminated some of the facets of the spiritual direction conversation and how it contributes to the experience of compassion and understanding in today's world.

Notes

1. See Norvene Vest ed., *Tending the Holy: Spiritual Direction Across Traditions* (Harrisburg: Morehouse Publishing, 2003). Vest describes both eastern and western practices of spiritual direction.

2. For a detailed understanding of the nature of spiritual direction, see William A. Barry and William J. Connolly, *The Practice of Spiritual Direction* (New York: HarperSanFrancisco, 1982) and Kathleen Fischer's, *Women at the Well: Feminist Perspectives on Spiritual Direction* (Maywah: Paulist Press, 1988).

3. Eileen P. O'Hea develops a picture of spiritual companionship in *In Wisdom's Kitchen: The Process of Spiritual Direction* (New York:The Continuum International Publishing Group Inc., 2000), 9.

4. The narrative is essential to spiritual direction. Janet Ruffing, RSM treats this in *To Tell the Sacred Tale: Spiritual Direction and Narrative*, (Mahwah: Paulist Press, 2011), pps. 20–22. In Chapter 3: "The Narrative Impulse in Human Experience," she describes the importance of this dimension of spiritual direction. See pages 68–92.

5. Elizabeth Liebert *In The Way of Discernment: Spiritual Practices for Decision Making* (Louisville: Westminster John Knox Press, 2008). Liebert defines contemplative listening and contemplative responding and links them to the process of discernment. See pages xix–xxi.

6. Lucy Abbott Tucker, ed., *Sacred Is the Call: Formation and Transformation in Spiritual Direction Programs* (New York: The Crossroad Publishing Company, 2005). In Chapter 10, "Embracing the Wisdom of the Body." Tucker discusses the relevance of paying attention to feelings and their significance in the spiritual direction conversation. See pages 101–109.

7. Maria Tattu Bowen, "Hearing with the Heart: Contemplative Listening in the Spiritual Direction Session," in Tucker Ibid. Bowen elaborates the facets of contemplative listening and all that it requires. See pages 33–41.

8. Mary Ann Scofield, "Waiting on God: Staying with Movements of God" and "Running from God: Resistance to the Movements of God," Tucker, Ibid. Scofield elaborates the essence of disscerning in respect to spiritual direction. See pages 52–67.

9. This is based on Maureen Conroy's contribution to this conversation. See *The Discerning Heart: Discovering a Personal God* (Chicago, Loyola University Press, 1993), 98.

10. The classical definitions provide a guide for spiritual directors and retreat directors in understanding the complexity of the inner dynamic of Movement and Countermovement. These definitions are developed as the Rules for the Discernment of Spirits in George E. Ganss, SJ, *The Spiritual Exercises of Saint Ignatius: A Translation and Commentary* (St. Louis, The institute of Jesuit sources, 1992), 121–128.

11. Ignatius of Loyola use the image of a "pointer of a scale in equilibrium" to describe the inner movement of the spiritual director but it can also be applied to the interior movement of the directee, as it is in this case. This is the fifteenth Annotation in *The Spiritual Exercises of St. Ignatius of Loyola*, Ibid. 25.

12. Fischer, pps. 53–74. Fischer develops this theme, particularly in her third chapter, "Women Experiencing and Naming God."

13. Mary Rose Bumpus and Rebecca Bradburn Langer, eds., *Supervision of Spiritual Directors: Engaging in Holy Mystery* (Harrisburg: Moorehouse Publishing, 2005). The authors provide a delightful description of this metaphor of the dance as it pertains to beginning spiritual directors in their chapter, "Supporting Beginning Directors: Participating in the Dance."

WORKS CITED

Buckley, Suzanne M., Ed. *Sacred is the Call: Formation and Transformation in Spiritual Direction Programs*. New York: The Crossroad Publishing Company, 2005.

Bumpus, Mary Rose, and Rebecca Bradburn Langer. *Supervision of Spiritual Directors: Engaging in Holy Mystery*. Harrisburg: Moorehouse Publishing, 2005.

Connolly, William A., and William J. Barry. *The Practice of Spiritual Direction*. New York: HarperCollins Publishers, 1982.

Conroy, Maureen, RSM. *The Discerning Heart: Discovering a Personal God*. Chicago: Loyola University Press, 1993.

Fischer, Kathleen. *Women at the Well: Feminist Perspectives on Spiritual Direction*. Mahwah: Paulist Press, 1988.

Liebert, Elizabeth. *The Way of Discernment: Spiritual Practices for Decision Making*. Louisville: Westminster John Knox Press, 2008.

O'Hea, Eileen P. *In Wisdom's Kitchen: The Process of Spiritual Direction*. New York: Continuum, 2000.

Ruffing, Janet K., RSM. *To Tell the Sacred Tale: Spiritual Direction and Narrative*. Mahwah: Paulist Press, 2011.

Vest, Norvene, Ed. *Tending the Holy: Spiritual Direction Across Traditions*. Harrisburg: Moorehouse Publishing, 2003.

CHAPTER SEVEN

Fear and Fundamentalism As Barriers to Civil Discourse

Nancy Porter

Personal belief and position as it relates to religion and politics are the underpinnings of fundamental choices people make in work, relationship, recreation, and idiopathic interests that have significant individual meaning. Father, however, advised us not to discuss them lest there be a verbal brawl at the Thanksgiving table. Deeply felt and, to the holder of the relevant beliefs, logically and utterly true, politics and religion are in different ways, grounded in philosophy and individual world view.

Civility in discourse seems increasingly rare, unfortunately. Civility implies restraint, tolerance, even politeness in considering contrary views of other individuals or groups. Social science research has provided abundant evidence that humans tend to develop powerful defenses around strongly held views and famously, political and religious belief systems, based on philosophy as much as fact, are carefully preserved and protected. Conservative and liberal worldviews have and continue to stand in pronounced and sometimes strident opposition to each other. This paper will seek to explore some of the barriers to civil discourse in current affairs, considering the nature of conservative and liberal worldviews, some surprising brain research which suggests some causation for the variance in attitudes between conservatives and liberals and finally, issues around the balance and potential imbalances between *mythos* and *logos* in religious and political perspectives.

Michael Laser in the December 6, 2010 *Christian Science Monitor* points out that the reason that little common ground is found on religious, political, and personal issues is that conservatives and liberals make logical arguments that are deeply felt which are based on arguments that are logical yet refutable. Ideally views from the right and left could inform each other but for individuals holding strongly to a conservative or liberal viewpoint, advancing and defending their worldview typically trumps most interest in consideration of views on the other side.

Conservative thinkers would argue for personal responsibility, that given the opportunity to support self and family, individuals can do so in this free society which offers equality under the law. What one earns is one's own and government intrusions into private dealings are harmful to the society in general. If one does not "make it" in this culture, it is on them. The legitimate job of government is to protect individuals and to provide a strong defense and national security (Laser, 2010).

Liberal thinkers would argue that we are not isolated individuals, that there are people who, due to a variety of personal and situational factors, cannot earn sufficient money to live reasonably and that there should be social safety nets to assure the less fortunate a decent life. Government rightly should oversee corporations to limit corruption, to solve problems that private institutions are not solving, and intervene in times of economic difficulty to assure employment. Discrimination on the basis of race, gender, religion, sexual orientation, class, and disability persists despite the law; recognition that it is not a level playing field is important in making policy decisions in government, education, and business (Laser, 2010).

Laser thoughtfully notes that both sides of the right/left continuum might realize that the opposing view offers some reasonable arguments that should be unconsidered. Civil discourse, the thoughtful exchange of opinions, is often absent in conservative/liberal discussion however. The strength of these positions in individuals at either end of the continuum seems foundational in the personality and is a factor which affects every aspect of their lives: their education, their relationships, and their religious and political affiliations.

Actor Colin Firth, while recently hosting a British TV show, suggested a lighthearted piece of research be undertaken which would explore whether the brains of self described liberals and conservatives were physically different. Two opposing political leaders plus ninety students who were self declared liberals or conservatives were analyzed through the use of MRI scans. The research was carried out by Geraint Rees director of the University College of London Institute of Cognitive Neuroscience and his associates and Rees related he was "very surprised" by the findings.

The 90 participants were given a likert scale test on which they confidentially evaluated their political preference—from "very liberal" to "very conservative."

The scientists used a sophisticated group of analyses to investigate the relationship between these numeric scores between one and five and gray matter volume. They found that increased gray matter in the anterior cingulated cortex was significantly associated with liberalism. There had been prior research that there had been a correlation between voting behavior and the amygdale across cultures and the scientists then proceeded to investigate their MRI data to evaluate whether there was a relationship between the gray matter volume of the amygdale and political attitudes. They found that increased gray matter volume in the right amygdale was significantly associated with conservatism. A replication study yielded the same results (Kanai, Feilden, Firth & Rees, 2011). The conclusions of the experiment are as follows:

> We speculate that the association of gray matter volume of the amygdala and anterior cingulate cortex with political attitudes that we observed may reflect emotional and cognitive traits of individuals that influence their inclination to certain political orientations. For example, our findings are consistent with the proposal that political orientation is associated with psychological processes for managing fear and uncertainty . The amygdala has many functions, including fear processing. Individuals with a large amygdala are more sensitive to fear, which, taken together with our findings, might suggest the testable hypothesis that individuals with larger amygdala are more inclined to integrate conservative views into their belief system. Similarly, it is striking that conservatives are more sensitive to disgust. . . . On the other hand, our finding of an association between anterior cingulate cortex volume and political attitudes may be linked with tolerance to uncertainty. One of the functions of the anterior cingulate cortex is to monitor uncertainty and conflicts. Thus, it is conceivable that individuals with a larger ACC have a higher capacity to tolerate uncertainty and conflicts, allowing them to accept more liberal views. (Kanai et al., 2011, p. 679)

Heightened awareness of potential danger and a tendency towards anxiety and fear would naturally orient an individual to safety, to familiarity. The description of basic conservative beliefs that preceded this focused on self preservation, the belief in capitalism and the marketplace, personal responsibility, and diminished social programs for those who can't make the grade. The ability to tolerate uncertainty and to support a larger government which would share resources to assure all a reasonable life would be a liberal view.

Historically, the dramatic changes that emanated from science and philosophy just as humans emerged from the Middle Ages were challenging to manage. The past hundred years, with unprecedented wars and bloodshed, the emergence of modern science, sociology, psychology and burgeoning technology offer adaptive challenges to each generation. For some, it was overwhelming and created an impetus to go back to the fundamentals of the Bible. Fundamentalism gained its strongest foothold and continued to grow in this country from the end of the 19th century to the present day.

FUNDAMENTALISM AND THE CLASH OF MYTH AND SCIENCE

Religion has typically been intertwined with government in cultures throughout the world. The United States of America was the first nation that was explicitly determined by its founders to be a secular state. Thomas Jefferson wrote that there should be a "wall of separation" between church and state and the First Amendment states, "Congress shall make no law respecting an establishment of religion, or prohibiting the free exercise thereof; or abridging the freedom of speech, or of the press; or the right of the people peaceably to assemble, and to petition the Government for a redress of grievances." The goal was a government of law that protected individual rights to spiritual and religious beliefs. As seemingly clear as the Constitution and its amendments are on this issue, there have been and continue to be challenges to determining the proper separation of these forces in this country or whether they should be separated at all.

The strict separation of church and state has not been widely favored by the citizenry since the founding of the country. The founding fathers, typically educated iconoclastic deists, did not represent the views of the people at large. Over the years since, through many changes and permutations, the connection of government and religion has not demonstrated total separation, but has many elements of overlap which would be in contrast to the Jefferson idea of a "wall." Presently, however, both Republican and Democratic parties identify either overtly or more subtly with religious faith. In the 2008 election, the more liberal Democratic party candidates were asked by a journalist to "describe their faith." It was not a question of whether they were people of faith, but made the assumption that they were. Obama and Clinton obliged, both espousing a Christian orientation. In the Republican Party, traditionally conservative in philosophy, there are entities and practices that are directly related to the Christian faith. George W. Bush's prayer meetings and organizations such as "The Family" whose influential political and corporate members gather together and collaborate on the basis of a common belief in Jesus are but two examples. It is difficult to imagine a serious candidate for president in this country today who is not a declared Christian. This flies in the face of what Jefferson and the other founders, largely deists, envisioned for the country and reflects the imbalance and overreach of religion into politics that had characterized the European countries they had left behind.

Nations that seek to disallow religion, such as the Soviet Union are doomed to fail in that effort. Nations that are theocratic can be abusive to citizens on the basis of religion rather than law. The separation of church and state envisioned for this country suggested a balance—a government of law and freedom of belief for all citizens. The implication is that a constitution, the balance of powers, and the ability to amend and interpret law as time goes on is the rational role of government. Religion, on the other hand, is belief, subjective by nature. It is easier to embrace the latter position if one sees the Bible and other religious stories as *mythos*—attempts to understand meaning, creation and the creator for the human.

Turning *mythos* into *logos*, declaring the Bible the inerrant word of God, or the "truth" paralyzes discussion and concretizes the position of the associated group. Fundamentalism is a feature of three major religions, Christianity, Judaism, and Islam, in that the metaphoric nature of the sacred texts is for these factions, fact and thus not debatable. In this country, two of the major motivators of a strong fundamentalist movement among Christians were the Copernican heliocentric theory and more significantly, the theory of evolution. Both of these scientific discoveries were interpreted as an affront to the centrality and importance of the human. They, in addition to other new formulations of the Western canon such as psychological and sociological notions of human society plus the rapidly changing technology which, among other things produced wars that slaughtered humans in numbers never imagined, created a fear in many and a desire to go back to "the fundamentals," the reassuring words of the New Testament that offered answers to human problems and salvation for believers.

Karen Armstrong, religious historian, portrays this as the challenge of placing myth and rational, empirical fact into their appropriate places. The Bible is seen by many Christians as a guide to life, not inerrant text. It supplies answers to the questions that cannot be addressed with scientific experiment and yet are vital to human life. As Armstrong says:

> Myth could not be demonstrated by rational proof; its insights were more intuitive, similar to those of art, music, poetry or sculpture. Myth only became a reality when it was embodied in cult, rituals, and ceremonies which worked aesthetically upon worshippers evoking within them a sense of sacred significance and enabling them to apprehend the deeper currents of existence. . . . Without a cult or mystical practice, the myths of religion would make no sense. They would remain abstract and seem incredible, in rather the same way as a musical score remains opaque to most of us and needs to be interpreted instrumentally before we can appreciate its beauty. (Armstrong, 2000, p. xvi)

Joseph Campbell considers that there are several functions of myth. The metaphysical function involves awakening a sense of awe at the mystery of being, something which no words can fully describe. The cosmological function seeks to connect ancient science to modern science. Sociologically, myths help to explain and maintain the social order and psychologically they guide individuals through the stages of life (Campbell, 1991). Myths are about meaning, not necessarily about fact. They are metaphoric; beneath the stories they tell are views of the origins of life and the sense of the culture in which people live. In illiterate cultures, they were rememberable. They were ways of sharing ideas of being which could be understood by individuals of all levels of intelligence and training. They provided stability to given cultures by creating shared notions of values and norms. Myths allowed a sense of awe and wonder at that which could not be "known." As science has taken the forefront in modern cultures and sensibilities, some would argue that the scarcity of vibrant myth today gives root to meaninglessness and estrangement, of nihilistic paradigms where there is painful lack of "meaning" to existence in current life.

Logic and science, empiricism in the form of *logos* stands in contrast to *mythos*. It is associated with fact and observable truth. *Logos* is the learning that helps people understand their environment, helps them to get things done. An empirically proven fact is hard to dismiss in credible fashion. It is the proof from the lab, the logic of the courtroom, the knowledge gained from hands-on experience. *Logos* cannot, however, explain the meaning of life. It cannot assuage human pain or sorrow or make sense of tragedy. Logos could not answer questions about the ultimate value of human life. This is the "preserve of myth and cult" (Armstrong, 2000, p. xvii).

The early days of the Enlightenment set in motion forces both in the church and in science that would challenge the status quo. Luther and Calvin challenged the dominance of the Roman Catholic Church and the theory of a heliocentric solar system fortified by the later evidence of Kepler and Galileo was a radical departure from the existing worldview that was threatening to some as it challenged the centrality of the human in the universe. Later, Sir Isaac Newton sought to purge Western society of myth which seemed primitive and passé. He could not recognize that the doctrine of the Trinity had been formulated by the Greek Orthodox theologians of the fourth century specifically as *mythos*. Father, Son, and Spirit were not objective facts but terms to express that which was "unnameable and unspeakable"—the divine (Armstrong, 2000). Francis Bacon felt that all truth must be subject to the empirical method and Renee Descartes also sought pure reason speaking always in the language of *logos*. The Enlightenment philosophers subscribed to a separation of church and state and embraced the logic of deism, rejecting the *mythos* of the older religious traditions.

Various factors in the 19th century caused some to try to merge *mythos* and *logos* in the interpretation of the Bible. The Civil War brought a level of death, destruction, and violence to a level not seen before in America. Some Christian preachers such as John Nelson Darby (1800–1882) spoke of the Apocalypse being imminent and the book of Revelation as being factual instead of metaphoric. He created the notion of the "Rapture," the literal reading of Revelations where the righteous would be lifted into heaven before the tribulation which would leave the sinners on earth to suffer for their transgressions (Armstrong, 2000).

Darwin's Theory of Evolution exacerbated the fear and distrust of the modern and the shock of an idea that, like Copernicus's Heliocentric Theory, again placed the human in a position of less importance in the grand scheme. The six thousand year old world, Adam and Eve, the message that the earth was given to the service of the human, all of this was thrown into doubt by these products of modern science. If Genesis was myth and not fact, perhaps Jonah was not in the belly of the whale, then perhaps Christ did not rise after three days. If one element of the Bible was shown to be errant, then what was a person to believe? The Scopes Trial pointed up the lack of rigor in the critique of evolutionary theory in the famous court battle between Clarence Darrow and William Jennings Bryant. A court ruling was not able to bend many Christian people's belief in the accuracy of the Bible as seen even today in the Dover, Pennsylvania trial where the right to teach creationism/intelligent design as science was disallowed. Opposition to the teaching of evolution continues on many fronts in this country.

The theory of evolution was seen very differently by conservative and liberal branches of the Christian tradition toward the end of the 19th century. Harriet Beecher Stow saw it as evidence of God's presence in every element of life—that evolution was a form of God showing love for his creation through his extraordinary design. For her and others, this would be a logical and constructive view of connections between science and faith.

Simplifying the multiplicity of possible interpretations of the Bible, the idea of Christian love, following the model of Jesus, motivating believers to help the less fortunate interpretation was supported by both conservative and liberal factions of the Christian church in the start of the 20th century. Taking interpretation of the message of the Bible further, however, in 1909, Charles Eliot, professor emeritus of Harvard University delivered an address titled "The Future of Religion" which portrayed a new Christianity which would have only one commandment which was the love of God in service to others. Theology would not be necessary nor would there be difficulty in accepting the views of other religions as the core element love and service could be generalized to all major religions. It would be a faith that focused on practice rather than doctrinal beliefs (Armstrong, 2000).

Eliot's words made logical sense to many in embracing the possibility that Christianity could be a uniting force between different belief groups. It was wise and reasonable to Eliot and similar minds that God could be seen as love, and evolution could stand beside a compliment a certain interpretation of the Bible, but was an extreme affront to the idea of fundamental Christianity seen through the eyes of some conservative Christians. For them, the Bible was inerrant, it was the word of God given to man through the Holy Spirit and was not to be modified or interpreted in such a simplistic manner. Scriptural inerrancy, the Virgin Birth of Christ, Christ's atonement for human sins on the cross, his resurrection, and the objective reality of his miracles were hard, non-negotiable truths for this group (Armstrong, 2000).

The split between the growing fundamentalist movement and the mainstream factions of Christianity grew only in the 20th century. The first and second world wars generated genocide, death, and destruction worldwide at a level never previously witnessed. The fact that Germany, one of the most cultivated societies in history, could unleash Hitler's devastation and the Holocaust defied rational explanation. It was followed closely by Hiroshima and Nagasaki and the Russian Gulag. The fearful apocalyptic visions this engendered and the desire for a world that reflected how "things should be" was a uniting force in creating fundamentalist countercultures. Following World War II, the Supreme Court ruled consistently against states sponsoring prayer in school and supported the IRS's rulings against institutions in the south that segregated white and black populations and did not permit inter-racial dating. Fundamentalists felt unfairly dominated by the liberal intellectual elite and strove to create their own religious and educational institutions that aligned themselves with their conventional, Biblical views of right and wrong (Armstrong, 2000).

The chaotic '60s only added to the energy of the fundamentalist movement. The 1979 Gallup Poll showed that one third of American adults who were polled considered they had had a "born again" experience. One half believed the Bible was inerrant and over 80 percent saw Jesus as divine. There were about 1300 evangelical Christian radio television stations with an audience of about 130 million and profits estimated in the billions (Lienesch, 1995). Jerry Falwell and his "Moral Majority," Tim LaHaye, and others began to feel their political strength. Pat Robertson said in one of his sermons, "We have together with the Protestants and Catholics enough votes to run this country and when the people say, 'We've had enough,' we are going to take over" (Harding, 1994, p. 70). Take that, Thomas Jefferson!

In 1978, The "Chicago Statement on Biblical Inerrancy" was produced at a summit of 300 evangelical scholars in Chicago. Barely departing from the original fundamentalist position statement of the early 20th century mentioned previously, the 1978 position reaffirmed the Bible as written by men through the Holy Spirit. "Holy Scripture . . . is of infallible divine authority in all matters upon which it touches . . . Being wholly and verbally God-given, Scripture is without error or fault in all its teachings . . . The authority of Scripture is inescapably impaired if this total divine inerrancy is in any way limited or disregarded or made relative to a view of truth contrary to the Bible's own" (Chicago Statement on Biblical Inerrancy, 1978).

The absolute surety and the potential political power of fundamentalist evangelicals and their institutions declined significantly in the 1980's with the scandals surrounding Jim and Tammy Faye Bakker and Jimmy Swaggart (Armstrong, 2000). Their entertainment-oriented and lowbrow preaching has evolved, however, into a variety of more sophisticated organizations that claim Jesus as their head and seek or command significant political power.

Fundamentalist organizations remain strong today, one of the most interesting being "The Fellowship" or "The Family" Jeff Sharlet, author and journalist, did extensive research on this organization including living within one of its compounds for a month. The Family was loosely organized in 1935 and opened to decision makers in this country to study the Bible and pray together. The well known National Prayer Breakfast is a feature of the organization each year and has been attended by numerous presidents including Barack Obama. Although it is a conservative organization and is populated mostly by Republicans, there are Democrats such as Hillary Clinton who have also attended the breakfast. It has been described as one of the most politically well-connected ministries in the world. The organization has become very quiet and "private" bordering on secretive in the past few years. Jeff Sharlet, in addition to living in one of the Family's compounds was able to investigate their archives before they were closed to public view.

Sharlet feels that the pulse of religious fundamentalism in this country has been and remains a prevailing force. "From Jonathan Edwards and the Revolutionary War that followed the First Great Awakening to the War on Terror, the theocratic strand has been woven into the American fabric, never quite dominant but always stronger and more enduring than those who imagine religion to be a personal, private affair realize" (Sharlett, 2008, p. 8).

Revisionist history was a convenient way to alter the meaning of Jefferson's "wall of separation" for fundamentalists from a range of eras. Karen Armstrong (2000) reports that John Whitehead, president of the conservative Rutherford Institute in the 1960's considered that the First Amendment had been grossly misread. He considered that the "wall" was meant to protect religion from the state, not vice versa. Jeff Sharlett's 2005 experience with the Family rendered the same opinion: "Federer (a Family leader), leaning over the back of his seat as several pastors bent their ears toward his story, wanted me to understand that what Jefferson—notorious deist and author of the Virginia Statute for Religious Freedom—had really meant to promote was a 'one way wall,' designed to protect the church from the state and not the other way around. Jefferson, Federer told me, was a believer and like all the Founders, he knew there could be no government without God. Why hadn't I been taught this? Because I was a victim of godless public schools" (Sharlet, 2005, p. 38). Federer later remarked to Sharlet, paraphrasing Orwell's *1984*, that "Those who control the present control the past" (Sharlet, 2005, p. 39).

The Family currently has a significant membership of individuals who are powerful political decision-makers. They identify as Christian, join together in meetings and retreats, support each other and believe that their highest calling and their common cause is to determine, in a sense, "what Jesus would do."

The figure of Jesus has always been subject to a myriad of interpretations. Though he is for many a symbol of forgiveness and non-violence, the antithesis of the Old Testament God of fear, Sharlet feels the Family has recast him as a warrior for righteousness, better suited to current events:

> Is "fundamentalism" too limited a word for a belief system of such scope and intimacy? Lately, some scholars prefer "maximalism," a term meant to convey the movement's ambition to conform every aspect of society to God. In contemporary America—from the Cold War to the Iraq War, the period of the current incarnation's Ascendency—that means a culture born again in the image of Jesus strong but tender, a warrior who hates the carnage he must cause, a man-god ordinary men will follow. . . . But I think "fundamentalism"—coined in 1920 as a self designation by those ready to do "battle royal for the fundamentals," hushed up now as too crude for today's chevaliers—still strikes closest to the movement's desire for a story that never changes, a story to redeem all that seems random, a rock upon which history can rise. (Sharlet, 2005, p. 38)

It is not difficult to imagine that Thomas Jefferson was very clear about what he meant by a "wall of separation" between church and state. It is the split between *mythos* and *logos*. Following the tradition of religious persecution and theocratic governments that characterized much of European history, the desire to create a secular state with religious freedom was logical. The government would be of laws, based on a Constitution that was amenable to change as history dictated—*logos*. On the other side of the wall, disconnected, was the right for people to freely engage in their chosen belief systems *mythos*. Laws would create control and freedom of religion would create an environment which would protect individual believers from persecution (so long as they obeyed the laws and didn't violate the rights of others). Imagining Jefferson's ideas as anything else—a one-way wall that protected religion from the state, for example, is irrational, self serving, and a distortion of Jefferson's idea.

Although the Scopes Trial and the passage of Roe vs. Wade have been major defeats for fundamentalist/evangelical movements, the movement remains strong—a force that is growing where mainstream churches are experiencing decline. The sheer force and certainty of belief is the piece that is problematic for the widespread acceptance of fundamentalism. Changing history to fit their philosophy of church and state is unconvincing to many on the "outside." Seeing the separation of church and state as working only one way—protecting religion from government is an example. R. Albert Mohler Jr., dean of the Southern Baptist Theological Seminary in Louisville, Ky. defies history when he contends that the founding fathers never wanted to exclude religion from public life which is why they cited God in national mottoes, "In God We Trust" (Masci, 2001). In truth, the motto was first used on a 2 cent coin in 1864, a 5 cent coin in 1866 and all American coins in 1938. "Under God" in the Pledge of Allegiance was added in 1954 and "In God We Trust" was legally adopted as the US national motto in 1954.

In consideration of the evangelical/fundamentalist perspective, however, the complete separation of church and state is almost impossible. It is difficult to imagine how one might separate one's own belief system from the work that they do. George W. Bush famously cited Jesus Christ as his favorite philosopher because he had "changed his heart." Issues such as abortion and gay rights create political schism in large part because they touch on individual belief systems that can't be judged as *logos*.

The thesis of this paper is that fundamentalism is a barrier to civil discourse in contemporary society. The problem, for the very religious right, is that the *mythos* of the Bible has been hardened into *logos*. Joseph Campbell said, "Every religion is true one way or another. It is true when understood metaphorically. But when it gets stuck in its own metaphors, interpreting them as facts, then you are in trouble" (Campbell, 1991). Why is it that the metaphoric nature of the Bible is taken to be immutable fact and what is the result of this view in public discourse today?

Life, with its mysteries, can elicit fear. Erich Fromm contended that we are thrust into life and then pulled out without any sense of why (Liebert & Spiegler, 1998). Making the religious word, in the case of American fundamentalism, the Bible, factual results in a "truth" which can ease some of the worry that comes from the ultimate ambiguity of life. It also creates a complete lack of ability to consider contrary views. "Fundamentalists have turned the *mythos* of their religion into *logos* either by insisting that their dogmas are scientifically true, or by transforming their complex mythology into a streamlined ideology" (Armstrong, 2000, p. 366).

Secular humanists, typically liberal in orientation, have their own intransigence, disallowing the intrusion of religion into legal or political venues however these viewpoints are typically engendered by the sort of rational philosophical positions that motivated the founding fathers to separate church and state. When *mythos* is turned into *logos*, there is no negotiation. When fundamentalist religion enters the political sphere, it has the hard-edged quality of rightness based on devotion to a belief system separated from science and empiricism. The political sphere in this country and others is always comprised of conservative and liberal perspectives seeking power and control. Negotiation is central to progress and the fervent, rigid, positions of fundamentalism are not subject to negotiation. If one knows the 'truth" that comes directly from God, there are no other options.

People at the far ends of the political spectrum will probably never be able to hear one another. Fundamentalist religion is an insult to rationality for many on the left and perhaps many in the center. H.L. Mencken, following the dismantling of William Jennings Bryan on the stand by Clarence Darrow in the 1925 Scopes trial, called fundamentalists "the scourge of the nation," "gaping primates of the upland valleys," and "yokels" (Armstrong, 2000, p. 177). Blind faith in metaphor is not credible to those who consider themselves rational thinkers. In the same breath, secular humanist belief, perhaps atheism at the extreme, are inflexibly opposed to myth and religion as credible resources and thus unacceptable to religious populations.

Perhaps the real debate and the potential "listening" moves toward the center as Laser had offered in the *Christian Science Monitor* article. Looking at history for guidance, it is apparent that freedom of religion needs to be upheld considering the destruction that can result from theocratic governments—think the Crusades, the Inquisition, human rights in Iran etc. It is probably more difficult for government to stay clear of religious influence. The Tea Party and conservative Republicans gain much energy from their constituents when they focus on the evils of abortion and gay marriage. Other issues of equal importance can move to the background when these "hot button" issues are brought forward. George W. Bush's campaign in 2000 and 2004 clearly took advantage of this.

History shows that a meshing of conservative and liberal thought can produce systems that work for their people. The free market embraces human initiative (conservative) but needs to be regulated (liberal). Social security, welfare, healthcare (liberal) for everyone can work if thoughtfully implemented and held to some level of fiscal responsibility (conservative). Experience has shown that negotiation can provide answers to vexing questions and that being flexible enough to negotiate is the vehicle that avoids gridlock and makes progress. All we need to do is listen.

REFERENCES

Armstrong, K. (2000). *The Battle For God*. Ballantine Books, New York City.

Campbell, J. (1991). *The Power of Myth*. Anchor Books, New York City.

Harding, S. (1994). "Imagining the Last Days: The Politics of Apocalyptic Language" in Martin E Marty and R. Scott Appleby (eds.), *Accounting for Fundamentalisms* (Chicago and London 1994), 70.

Kanai, R., Feilden, T., Firth, C. & Rees, G. (2011). Political Orientations are Correlated with Brain Structure in Young Adults. *Current Biology*, 21, Issue 8, 677–680.

Laser, M. (2010). Conservatives vs. Liberals: Neither Side Owns the Truth. *Christian Science Monitor*, Volume 103, Issue 2.

Liebert, R. & Spiegler, R. (1998). *Personality, Strategies and Issues*. Brooks/Cole Publishing Company, New York City.

Lienesch, M. (1998). *Redeeming America: Piety and Politics in the New Christian Right*. Chapel Hill, N.C.

Sharlet, J. (2006). Through a glass, darkly: How the Christian Right is Reimagining U.S. History. *Harpers Magazine*, December 2006.

Sharlet, J. (2008). *The Family. The Secret Fundamentalism at the Heart of American Power*. Harper Perennial, New York City.

Sharlet, J. (2010). *C Street: The Fundamentalist Threat to American Democracy*. Little, Brown and Company, New York City.

CHAPTER EIGHT

Lessons From the Ecumenical Lifeworld: Dialogue and Civility

Steven Guerriero

This essay is based on my research of Roman Catholic ecumenists and a study of their lifeworld. The research was conducted in the mid-nineteen nineties, a period of time that I would describe as the "Indian summer" of ecumenism. Today as we are into our second decade of the twenty-first century we find ourselves in the heart of an ecumenical winter. The word *ecumenism* shares the same Greek origin as economics and ecology. The root word *oikos* means house or to inhabit, and *oikoumene* means general, universal or the inhabited world. The terms ecumenism, ecumenical and ecumenist have been associated through the twentieth century with the worldwide movement of Christian churches toward a search for unity. Why is a study of the ecumenical lifeworld valuable? The ecumenist, using open systems terminology, is a boundary spanner, moving within a world of organizational and faith systems. We discover in the narrative accounts an ability to communicate effectively and authentically across interpersonal and inter-organizational boundaries, embracing the diversity in other faith traditions in a creative, respectful and loving manner. If we look beyond the ecumenical domain, the lessons we learn from these individuals have wide systemic implications in meeting the challenge of dysfunctional attitudes and behaviors that are chronic sources of conflict and barriers to any type of civil discourse and problem solving. I chose to study these ecumenists for several reasons that include my own interest and participation in ecumenical work at the diocesan and parish level. In addition it was clear, if I wanted to study system boundaries and people who span them what better choice than study people crossing the boundaries of faith. There is a reason for the old adage not to talk religion or politics at a party. Religion and politics carry deep convictions and deeper divisions. It was evident to me that by studying these ecumenists I would likely find some of the most challenging situations and emotional response.

As an educator and organizational consultant for the last twenty-five years, dialogue has and continues to be the most useful process I have found to constructively work through difficult issues and positions that create barriers to individual and organizational learning and effectiveness. The individuals who have influenced my thinking the most in the area of dialogue are the late theoretical physicist, David Bohm (1990) and others who have followed his lead including, Peter Senge (1990), Linda Ellinor and Glenna Gerard (1998) and William Isaacs (1999). True dialogue, as they describe, requires the ability to bracket our own assumptions in order to listen with a spirit of openness and understanding. Bohm describes the essential nature of dialogue as consistent with its Greek origins, "*dia*" and "*logos*," which literally means *through the word*. Dialogue is distinguished by reciprocity and a symmetric flow of communication, uncharacteristic of our typical asymmetric discussion that is frequently marked by a power differential (Habermas, 1984). The art of dialogue involves a balance of inquiry and advocacy. The goal is not to convince, cajole or coerce. The goal is to create a space, a place of common ground, where meaning can be shared. These skills can be learned but are not easily applied in a cultural context that still favors debate and winning, usually at all cost.

Today we live in a society, and a political culture in particular, that seems completely devoid of dialogue and any standard of civil discourse. Unfortunately this polarization in America is not new. Unless we have fallen into the nostalgia trap or forgotten our history, we know that what is going on now is merely a continuation with enhancement of the rancorous and divisive discourse that has been part of the American scene from its founding. In retrospect, it reached a full crescendo in the decades running up to the Civil War, rang loud and clear over the hard and soft money debates of the late nineteenth century and as many of us know from first-hand experience ripped through the country during the Civil Rights movement of the nineteen sixties, the protests over the Vietnam War and the Watergate era. No, the lack of civility in public discourse is not new, just being perfected at present stoked by the presence of twenty-four hour news, talk radio, social networking and obscenely financed special interests. This speed and dissemination of information allows little time for thought or reflection. In this context it begs the question can there be any true dialogue? Is civil discourse just an idealized construct, an abstraction that is so far removed from reality that is held out but never achieved? I would like to believe that the answer to both questions is no. The thoughts presented in the essay that follows may explain why.

The study of the ecumenical lifeworld yields insight into the qualities and conditions that enable a culture of understanding, respect and civility. The greatest legacy of these ecumenists may not be in what they accomplished, as remarkable as it has been considering all the obstacles and lack of reception on the part of the institutional Church. I believe their greatest legacy is in how they did it. The purpose of this essay is to trace the *how* of their work and what it means. It begins with a historical perspective of the ecumenical lifeworld, the description of several key concepts and a brief description of the participants.

The modern ecumenical movement is an artifact of the twentieth century beginning in the first half of the century with Protestant and Orthodox churches in dialogue primarily focused on sociopolitical and economic matters. With time the conversations expanded beyond peace and social justice to include a shared interest in biblical scholarship and theological issues. The active participation of the Roman Catholics officially waited until the doors of the church opened with Vatican II. The historical context of the Catholic entry on the ecumenical scene and the subsequent decades of the twentieth century are critical to understanding just how challenging the ecumenical lifeworld has been for these Roman Catholic ecumenists. All of the participants except one were born into the pre-Vatican II church. During much of the first half of the twentieth century while the Protestant and Orthodox churches were trying to overcome centuries of distrust and lack of cooperation, the Roman Church was doing all it could to avoid it. After all as Kelly (1990) describes, Catholicism felt no need to cooperate or seek ways of greater unity with Protestants who were heretics and the Orthodox who were schismactics. Papal Encyclicals of Pius XI, *Mortalium Animos* (1928) and Pius XII *Mystici Corporis* (1943) and Humani Generis (1950) all reinforce that the only way to unity was returning to the one true church.

While there was growing informal or behind the scenes work by individuals in the Church during the late nineteen forties and fifties, the official position of the Roman Catholic Church on ecumenism did not change significantly until the pontificate of John XXIII beginning in 1958. On Pentecost Sunday June 5, 1960 John XXIII instituted the Secretariat for Promoting Christian Unity (SPCU). In preparation for a General Council of the Church, John XXIII promulgated the Papal Constitution, *Humanae Salutis* on December 25, 1961, that acknowledged and rejoiced at the anticipated participation of the Protestant churches in the Second Vatican Council, which convened the following October, 1962. The Council's decree on ecumenism, *Unitas Redintregratio* and other Vatican II and post-councilor documents carried the message of unity and reconciliation. As the decades followed the individuals referenced in this essay immersed themselves in the work of ecumenism. It is important to note that the differences between liberal and conservatives in the Church that were apparent before and during the Council widened further in the decades that followed. It is not uncommon to have swings in ideological thinking in any political or quasi-political organization or society. The hope is that there may be a more balanced or moderate perspective that prevails against the extremes. There is little question that in the decades following the Council the conservative response strengthened. Like the gradual narrowing of a blood vessel, the ecumenical spirit so vibrant in the immediate glow of Vatican II became more and more constricted. In spite of John Paul II's Encyclical on Christian unity *Ut Unum Sint* in 1995, the reality on the ground was different. There was stronger skepticism, a growing lack of serious ecumenical priority in dioceses and parishes and outright resistance from the Church to significant areas of theological convergence that were emerging in ecumenical dialogue among mainline Christian churches. This was the climate these ecumenists found themselves.

The Church, like all organizations, is a living system. All systems have boundaries to define and demarcate themselves. In a mechanical system the boundaries are highly structured and rigid in order to maintain a fixed operational integrity. In living systems, human, social and ecological, boundaries are not only for protection but are actually the points of relationship with the external environment. The boundary is the frontier of interrelationship and interdependence. The boundary needs to be permeable. In an organization this means some individuals must be boundary spanners, having the ability to bridge their own system with others. If an organization is going to exist and thrive in a complex interdependent environment it needs the active exchange of ideas, knowledge, energy and resources. Robert Miles (1980) wrote extensively about organizational boundaries and some of the inherent challenges in managing those boundaries. It requires having one foot in your own camp and one in someone else's. The boundary is filled with opportunity and threat. You may be seen with suspicion in your own organization as well as with the groups you are trying to connect. The ability to live in this dynamic tension is not easy. The role conflict and ambiguity the boundary spanner feels will vary depending on how open or closed their organizational system is. A closed system that operates off very black and white assumptions and takes action accordingly is probably going to be highly defensive in its posture to any disconfirming information that is presented. The response is generally exerting more control and tightening the boundary. The more open the system the greater the opportunity there is to turn the black and white into shades of gray. This opening, however slight, indicates some desire and value in engaging with and understanding the other. Boundary spanners, just as leaders, need a high level of communicative competency (Habermas, 1984) as well as emotional intelligence (Goleman, 1995) if they are to be successful. Ecumenists standout as exemplars of boundary spanning with their skills in dialogue, respect and civility.

In addition to the nature of dialogue and the historical and systems context of ecumenism, there are two other concepts that are critical to understanding this study; they are meaning-making and the lifeworld. Meaning-making is a dynamic process. Social phenomenologist Alfred Schutz (1970) described meaning-making as an intentional process that only becomes apparent in reflection and does not exist in prephenomenial experience. It is a shared experience in the intersubjective world of *self* and *other*. Meaning-making is described by the early social constructionists, Peter Berger and Thomas Luckmann (1967) "as an ongoing correspondence between my meanings and their meanings in this world, that we share a common sense about reality" (p. 23). It is through this shared understanding of meaning that the process of communication and mutuality becomes possible (Habermas, 1971). Meaning-making is a personal and shared activity that occurs in the lifeworld. The lifeworld is a term that was first used in phenomenology by Husserl (1970) to describe a pretheoretical and prereflective attitude. It was Schutz (1970) who reshaped Husserl's conception of the lifeworld into a social and cultural context in his social phenomenology. The lifeworld in Schutzian terms is the *world of daily living*. Habermas (1987) describes the lifeworld as a shared social construct, which is created through the communicative process. The ecumenical lifeworld is built on shared experiences interpreted through the individual lens of faith development and the relationships established through communicative action. The lifeworld is our door into the lives of the participants described in this essay. We discover their lifeworld through our ability to connect with and interpret the phenomena as experienced by the other. Bentz (1989) describes this process, which is both epistemological and methodological, as interpretive sociology or hermeneutic-phenomenology. What we find in this lifeworld are distinctive images in their words that emerge from the narratives describing their lived experience. The image of spirituality has a particular connection to the patience and perseverance they practiced.

The individuals chosen for this study were experienced in ecumenical affairs. They were selected from a pool of nominees that was submitted by four nominators, people recognized as active leaders in the ecumenical movement. Participation was voluntary and the final selection for the study was based on the desire to create a balance in gender, age and experience. There was a mix of clergy, religious and lay-people. The variety of roles represented included diocesan ecumenical positions, parish or community ecumenical roles, theologians and academics. The participants had diverse family backgrounds, educational experiences and represented a significant range in their age. Over the course of eighteen months I conducted in-depth interviews and follow-up conversations with the participants. They were asked to describe their earliest memories of difference and diversity. Next, they explored any influencing factors, including people, events or personal experiences that may have been significant moments on their ecumenical journey. Finally, they shared what sustained them in their work. Their narratives present fascinating stories and important insights into how they developed their ecumenical worldview. It is a story of individuals who often from an early age dared to question and take risks in challenging their own assumptions and those that were placed upon them by their church and wider culture. Their stories were deconstructed and organized thematically into five categories: images of ecumenism, family environment and influence, educational experiences, faith development and spirituality, and living the vision of ecumenism.

The participants' images of ecumenism provide a cognitive, affective and spiritual window into their understanding and meaning-making in the ecumenical lifeworld. Words like inclusive, dialogue, exploration, risk, pain, conversion, repentance, healing, patience and perseverance fill their narratives. Their image of Christian unity is not monolithic and monarchial. Their voices often echoed one of their acknowledged heroes, Augustin Cardinal Bea. Bea, the first chair of the Secretariat for Promoting Christian Unity, frequently used the image of ecumenism as *unity not uniformity*. Uniformity expresses compliance, control and a static condition. Unity expresses relationship, interdependence and strength in diversity. This unity is described in the ecumenical world as *koinonia*, a Greek word that expresses an existing communion, unity or wholeness, albeit not fully visible. Michael Kinnamon (1993) described *koinonia* as focusing on our oneness not separateness, on relationship more than institutional structures. Kinnamon further states that *koinonia* was a recurring theme in Saint Paul's teaching as affirming diversity as a constitutive element in the mystical body of Christ.

The image that surfaced most frequently and is so closely identified with the interpersonal nature of the ecumenical lifeworld is dialogue. The healthy internal dialogue that is present in all these individuals through their self-concept and acceptance is manifest interpersonally in a communicative process that is marked by mutuality and respect. I never once heard from any participant anything that resembled the expression, "mine is better than yours." Dialogue does not mean we agree on everything nor do we give up our own values. It means we are able to bracket our assumptions and positions in order to fully hear and understand the voice of the other. This is how common ground is developed.

The ecumenical lifeworld is not an idyllic place free from the pains of human struggle. The ecumenical movement was born in pain, a pain that suffers from the lost unity in the body of Christ. This pain is manifest in the individual lives of the ecumenists in unpleasant memories of unsuccessful attempts to bridge the chasm of Christian traditions. Whether the pain is from a marriage or family relationship, the feelings of being marginalized in one's own faith community or the multiple taboos of Catholics and Protestants that have perpetuated stereotypes and mistrust, pain is a reality in this lifeworld and one that needs constant healing and reconciliation.

The influence of the family environment, both immediate and extended, is a common theme among the participants. The significant aspects of the family environment constellate around three specific themes: self-awareness and acceptance of one's own differences, promoting tolerance and appreciation for differences, and the dynamics of mixed (ecumenical) marriages. It is important to note that these participants came from very diverse family backgrounds representing the mosaic of the American family in the nineteen fifties and sixties from working class to middle class. These were not made for television families; they were real with all the trials and tribulations that go with family life. While there was a wide range of economic, educational and social distinction in their backgrounds, there were strong similarities in their experience and message about self and other.

The ecumenical lifeworld begins with self-knowledge and self-recognition. Acceptance of self opens the heart and mind to accept others. To illustrate this, we see that many of the participants recognized their life circumstances as economically or socially disadvantaged in relation to their Protestant neighbors. This did not evoke envy or hostility. They accepted this in quiet appreciation for themselves, as well as being open to others. One Africa-American participant found what it was like to be a minority within a minority. Not only did this individual have to endure the segregation in an all black school in the rural south, but to be the only Black Catholic in the school. While subjected to the pain of name calling and cruel teasing by her own race and living the institutionalized separate but equal, this did not deter her from her own convictions and sense of self.

Parental models of tolerance and respect may be one of the most critical factors, particularly in the period these participants were coming of age. Many families were active in the Civil Rights movement. Other families felt the stigma from difference in social class or ethnic origin. The message these young children received was respect for difference even when it was staring you down. It was not an easy road but through it all these individuals seemed to emerge with sense of self-worth and dignity.

Half of the individuals in this study experienced the dynamics of mixed or ecumenical marriages. These experiences, which ultimately led to greater understanding, were not without difficulty and pain. One participant, a Catholic priest, described growing up with an Episcopalian father and a Catholic mother. He recounted an epiphany for him that happened in fifth grade. He remembered coming home with the Baltimore Catechism in-hand shaken and upset to learn his father would not be with them in heaven. This was only one of the many problematic and theologically inaccurate statements in this text that was the principal tool of instruction for a whole generation of young Catholics. His mother, he said smiling warmly, was the first ecumenist he met. She interpreted the doctrine more broadly and inclusively easing his mind and preparing him in a small way for his own adult reception of ecumenical ideas.

The ability to question and discern is remarkable in these children and young adults. One individual commented how crazy it was that he could not belong to the YMCA and use the pool because Protestants swam in the water. Another participant said she could never join in on the not so friendly snowball fights between Protestant and Catholic school kids as they waited across the road from each other for their respective buses. Their stories speak to a life journey where understanding the other is inseparable from one's own personal growth in knowledge, reasoning and spirit. This may partially explain why these individuals, even in their early years, seem to be able to separate the cultural messages that divide rather than build community. The expression of becoming more fully human marks this lifeworld and expresses both the importance of self-recognition and the humility of self-limitation, appreciating the self and other. It is the cornerstone of inclusion because if we are willing to acknowledge our own strengths and limitations (as expressed in our faith tradition) we open ourselves up to the recognition and reconciliation required to span the boundaries of different faith traditions.

If forming a mature concept of self and other is fundamental to the individual in the ecumenical lifeworld, a thirst for knowledge is closely behind. In all of the narratives there is a restless quality in the ecumenists' desire to move beyond the status quo. As several participants expressed, there is always a need to seek knowledge and be critical of those who feel they have cornered the market on truth. Like their diverse economic backgrounds, these future ecumenists had very different educational experiences yet surprisingly ended up with a similar openness to people of other faith traditions. A number of participants recalled their first real encounter with Protestants or other faith traditions was in school. These learning environments, particularly at the university level, were open to critical thinking and reflection creating opportunities to explore and question many assumptions about life and faith. This avid curiosity seemed to be a product of both home and school environments in many cases, while these participants were still quite young.

The availability to be open to learn and grow is not confined to the halls of academe. It is a life choice, to encounter new and diverse ideas, places and people with acceptance. It is about taking risks and exploring even when your own faith community looks at you with skepticism or mistrust. One participant's comment emphasizes this point; "to be faithful means you must work to reform and renew your church in the present. It is not disloyal or unfaithful to critique that which you love." When you can be self-critical, you open the opportunity to hear other voices, voices of change. Developing a critical consciousness also helps discover the institutional shortcomings any organization, religious or secular, has in its history.

The ecumenical lifeworld is surrounded by a deep sense of spirituality that has nourished the individual and collective paths of the people doing this work. In their minds there is no separation from being ecumenical and being spiritual. Ecumenism is not an option for them; it is what it means to be fully Christian. One cannot live the gospel message without being ecumenical. The spirituality that permeates their lives is manifest in many forms of piety from prayer and communal worship to researching the depths of theological questions. It is spirituality, appropriately labeled, for the long haul with patience and perseverance. One participant summed it up so completely when asked how she felt about her work as a theologian and the progress made toward convergence of critical theological questions like Baptism, Eucharist and Ministry. In response to her acknowledgement of the Roman Catholic Church's resistance to the reception of these theological breakthroughs she said: "I must realize that every day when I come to work, the work I am doing may never be realized in my lifetime." I wondered then and still do, how many people could say that? This was their ecumenical lifeworld held together by self-acceptance, inclusive behavior, a quest for knowledge and an abiding spirit that guided them every day.

The narratives reveal many provocative insights and posit questions as to how we might understand why certain individuals are able to effectively engage in dialogue across differences. At the completion of the original study I constructed a model of ecumenical praxis. I used the word praxis for a specific reason. Praxis is a term commonly used in the relational constructs of systems thinking, the emancipatory language of Critical Theory, and Participatory Action Research. It is a process of thought, action, and reflection. The emancipatory quality inherent in praxis is from its early use in Marxist circles, particularly in the writing of Antonio Gramsci. Gramsci (1971) talked about the philosophy of praxis being rooted in the popular masses, as a challenge to embedded ideology and a vehicle to educate the common people. According to Paulo Freire (1970;1973), praxis involves a fundamental shift of mind and heart, which is open to dialogue and critical consciousness for the purpose of eliminating oppression. Praxis in the ecumenical lifeworld describes the convergence of the ontological and teleological, being and intentionality. This convergence was stated consistently across the participants when asked to respond to the question; is being ecumenical something we are or something we do? The answer was both, there is no separation.

The original model was developed around three conceptual domains: cognitive & faith development (post-formal dialectical thinking and reasoning), social phenomenology (intrinsic relevance and self-typification) and spirituality (ecumenical spirituality). The purpose was to overlay conceptual frameworks on the narratives in order to better understand the meaning of the ecumenical lifeworld and creative ways to encourage the recognition and reception of ecumenical work. Unfortunately the recognition and reception of ecumenism did not flourish in the Catholic Church. The model of praxis in reflection and perspective still holds valuable lessons in providing insight into the dynamics of dialoguing across diversity. Expanding the model today takes into account how we might apply the lessons learned from these ecumenists to our present culture that desperately needs the ability to restore perspective, balance and civility to the polarizing, ideological divides we face at home and abroad.

The theoretical frameworks of developmental psychology, specifically adult faith development, provide a lens through which we are able to identify an individual's readiness to embrace levels of complexity in one's life. This speaks to an ability to hold the dialectical tension of differences and the changing dynamics of meaning-making. The theories examined are from James Fowler (1981;1984) and Sharon Parks (1986;2000). Their models are variants of stage development theory influenced among others by the works of Piaget, Perry, Kohlberg and Gilligan.

Fowler echoes a common theme of faith development, which starts with an important premise: Faith is a human universal. While the manifestations of faith may differ among humankind, the essential qualities and questions that faith possesses are surprisingly similar. Fowler (1984) states "We do not live long or well without meaning. That is to say, we are creatures who live by faith" (p. 50). Fowler's model is composed of seven stages built on a process of succession from less to more complex levels of reasoning and values. Fowler, as with other constructive developmentalists, would agree stages are not clean breaks or a defined ladder that one climbs from one life phase to another. The stages do reflect epistemological and axiological changes that influence our understanding of self and others. When an adolescent enters the early stages of formal operational thinking, which Fowler calls synthetic/conventional, there is a growing ability to synthesize knowledge, abstract ideas and concepts. It is important to note that Fowler uses the word synthetic as meaning synthesis not artificial. The word conventional implies that the knowledge and ideas synthesized are coming primarily from significant others and familiar institutions like family, school and church. Fowler comments that many individuals become embedded or equilibrate at the stage of synthetic/conventional faith, because they find it difficult to move beyond the values and beliefs that have become internalized and affirmed by outside authority. They have yet to develop a critical consciousness and reflective response to the tacit givens in their life. When we think of the strong fundamentalist and rigidly ideological positions today across many faith traditions and their political and social expressions, we understand the value of Fowler's insight into why many people are caught in these polarized positions.

Fowler's fifth stage is individuative/ reflective faith and ushers in the neo-Piagetian full formal operations of cognition. He explains two key aspects of individuative-reflective faith chronologically tied to the maturation processes of early adulthood. First is an affirmation in self-authorization, moving out from behind the masks of roles and expectations. The second feature is the ability to challenge the beliefs and values tacitly held from the prior stage. This critical process leads to a greater sense of self-ownership, commitment and accountability to explicit beliefs and values. In looking at the narratives in this study it seems possible that the participants either entered Fowler's individuative/reflective stage earlier in adolescence or as Parks (2000) will posit there is a transitional phase. They clearly had the ability to critique much of the conventional thinking around them.

Fowler's sixth stage is conjunctive faith, a process that emerges in mid-life and beyond. It is a post-formal operational stage that is functionally dialectical. This is the time when we become more fully aware of the contradictions and polarities of our self, society, and our expressions of the ultimate. It is at this midpoint of life that we recognize the nature of being young and old, masculine and feminine, generative and self-destructive, and the need to hold these tensions together at one time. The notion of truth is no longer thought of in terms of a linear construct or an absolute. It is a multi-formed concept, which in its paradox and ambiguity actually yields a new richness in truth. Conjunctive faith inaugurates a new awareness and appreciation for not only the myths and stories of our faith, but for other faiths around us. Fowler (1984) describes this not as simple relativism but "a disciplined openness to truths of those who are 'other,' based on the experience of a deep and particular commitment to one's own tradition . . . [and] the humility that knows that the grasp on ultimate truth that any of our traditions can offer needs continual correction and challenge" (p. 66). Individuals at the stage of conjunctive faith will often be questioned or challenged as "unbelievers" by those in the community who are at less critical stage of faith.

The process of faith development finds completion in Fowler's model in "universalizing faith," a stage which heralds a decentration of self in both an epistemological and axiological for valuation sense. Epistemologically this stage is built on widening circles of "perspective taking" that starts as early as the mythic-literal stage. It reaches its culmination in universalizing faith, in one's ability to fully know the world through the eyes of the other. Likewise, the values we have professed through development are now fully committed, because they give our lives meaning. This commitment is focused on the relationship of universal love and justice, and our actions support these values by working against oppression, violence, and division. There is oneness with the power of the divine.

Sharon Parks (1986; 2000) describes the journey toward adult faith as three distinct yet integrated domains of cognition, dependence, and community. Cognition addresses how one thinks about composing meaning at a given stage of faith. Dependence describes how one feels (affect) in the meaning-making process understanding that dependence can mean both "being held" as subject and to "holding on to" (as object). Finally, community represents the individual's development of social awareness and acceptance. These three domains move through four stages, adolescent/conventional, young adult, tested adult and mature adult.

Parks' model, while having many similarities to Fowler's, also offers some different perspectives. As noted above, Parks observed through her work with college age students that there was a unique stage between adolescent/conventional (synthetic/conventional) and tested adult (individuative/reflective). She identified this transition period as a unique time when the post-adolescent is claiming more self awareness around their responsibility and intentionality. It is a time of more thoughtful critique with differing positions from the authority bounded conventional stage. It is not simply the counter-dependent push back.

Another important contribution of Parks is tracing the evolving beliefs, attitudes and behaviors around community across the developmental journey. Community, this perfectly human need for belonging, can enable or constrain self-awareness and development. The conventional community draws its strength from authority and dependency. It sets a clear boundary between us and them. The demarcation may be based on any number of differences from race and ethnicity to religion and politics. Boundary spanning in a conventional community is seen primarily as a defensive role, protecting the community from the encroachment of new or disconfirming ideas or information. In a highly controlled organization or social system declaring one's own inner dependence is a risky business. Sanctions may be very high. Personal and group development goes through various phases of differentiation and integration; it is a natural oscillation. The hope is for a balance where one can feel inclusion and independence without sacrificing either.

The diffuse community that Parks describes is the area of transition where the expansion of experience brings new ideas, people and opportunities. This corresponds to the ecumenists' journey with specific regard to their educational encounters as young adults at university and seminary. The nature of community becomes self-selecting as both Parks and Fowler describe but based on criteria the young adult is shaping and revising continually.

The mentoring community is one that directly relates to the ecumenists in this study. Many of the participants spoke of the critical role mentors played in their formation. Mentoring provides an important life-line of knowledge and belonging as the individual is charting new territory. Mentoring not only provides the individual with one-on-one support. A mentoring community opens a wider range of social networks fostering the development of new and diverse communities. It represents the most inclusive stage in the maturation process of adult faith. This form of community recognizes the intrinsic value of relationships that are grounded in interdependence and openness to the other.

The narratives reveal many provocative insights into the developmental process, particularly the ability to move beyond formal operations. One constitutive factor of post-formal development that is critical for understanding the nature of meaning-making is the ability to think and process dialectically. Michael Basseches (1984) has conducted research and written extensively on dialectical thinking. I have summarized some of the points of his schemata of characteristics that can be identified as post-formal dialectical. Dialectical thinking is multi-relational, rather than linear or dichotomous. It spans individual systems or is meta-systematic. Dialectical thinking is evident where knowledge seeking behavior embraces contradictions and polar tension creatively and an essential factor in understanding the process of change.

It seems evident the participants in this study all demonstrated an ability to think dialectically reaching at mid-life what Kegan (1994) describes as a fourth level of consciousness, a post-formal, meta-systematic view. Post-formal dialectical thinking is possible because the individuals are available to embrace an epistemology that is relational rather than causal. Becoming adult in your faith does not happen unless as one participant noted, "you have the ability to shake off undifferentiated views." This means challenging the beliefs and values we have tacitly held, and the mental models (Senge, 1990) constructed from these assumptions that direct our behavior. Accomplishing this is no easy task, especially if you are in a community that looks suspiciously on individuals who challenge the status quo. The concept of mental models is the link between the domain of cognitive development and the social construction of the ecumenical lifeworld. Mental models (Senge, 1990; Argyris, 1990) may be described as our perceptions, assumptions and beliefs about how the world works around us. These mental models form the basis of our attitudes and behaviors and ultimately shape the course of our actions.

In the original model of "ecumenical praxis" there were two factors from Schutz's social phenomenology of the lifeworld, "typification" and "relevance" that seemed to speak to the ability of the participants to critique the messages and experiences around them. Their lifeworld as described earlier is an intersubjective world, where interpretation of experience is based on a stock of common knowledge that underpins the understanding, meaning-making and beliefs in daily life.

At an early age these meanings are constructed through our primary institutions of socialization, the family, the community and the organizations that support them. Our first mental models are created from these experiences. We anticipate or expect typical styles and forms to be manifest, in our experiences in the physical and social world. The typical styles are referred to by Schutz as typifications. They are the product of a history of socio-cultural interactions. In other words, we expect a certain response based on what the culture or others have previously told us. When we do not receive the expected response we can either take a defensive position of blocking the disconfirming information or we can begin to question our own assumptions. We know from the stages of development described earlier that individuals who are embedded in the synthetic/conventional or authority/bound stage will find it difficult to be critical since the typifications of any given social group reflect the dominant cultural norms and patterns of behavior. The greater challenge is when an individual or group becomes more and more selective about what is allows to process as new information. Argyris (1990) describes this pattern of response as the "ladder of inference." The ladder represents our mental pathway that travels through multiple layers of process from our observations and experiences to our decision to take action. Along this pathway we are selecting or filtering the information we take in and assigning some meaning to it based on our personal or socio-cultural perspective. At the point of meaning-making we begin to form assumptions and draw conclusions that lead to certain beliefs we have about our lifeworld. It is based on these beliefs that we take action. This process as you might imagine does not take hours or weeks of deliberation. Generally the time it takes us to run up the ladder of inference is a split-second. This mental pathway can be limiting and self-sealing or potentially expansive depending on how we choose to use it. What Argyris sees as problematic in the ladder is a reflexive loop that develops between our beliefs and what we select from our experience. When our beliefs continually serve as the criteria for our selection of incoming information our choices are narrowed and the mental model we have constructed becomes self-sealing. This means no new information can be processed and we continue individually and/or collectively to take action on greater abstractions that constellate in our beliefs. The way we challenge the assumptions of mental models is in our ability to reflect on them in real time questioning the perceptions that form beliefs and actions.

This ability to challenge one's mental models is informed by what Schutz described as self-typification and intrinsic relevance. Since typifications become embedded in the common language of the social group, they lend a strong bias against challenges to how the social order typifies. In order to challenge this individuals or groups must develop the ability to self-typify. This ability was apparent in the participants' adolescent development most commonly in how they rejected the hurtful exchange of typifications or stereotypes used by Roman Catholics and Protestants. They were able to self-typify over and above what a wider cultural context was telling them. This, in essence, creates a new set of collective typifications in the ecumenical world that guide a very different pattern of thought and behavior.

Along with self-typification these individuals were able to establish another critical step in determining what in their social lifeworld was relevant and what was not. Schutz described four different zones of relevance but for our purposes here the focus will be on the distinction he makes between imposed and intrinsic relevance. Imposed relevance from an individual or group is thought or action that is beyond our control, and while it is imposed upon us, we may not see it as being in our best interest. Intrinsic relevance is the product of our interests, which have emerged from our conscious choice of a particular thought, goal or action. When relevance is imposed, and in many cases not clearly supported by those effected by the imposition, one may expect to see resistance, alienation and defection from the imposing group.

We have at this point a picture of individuals who have the ability to reason dialectically and are comfortable with questioning their own mental models and those that are imposed upon them. What we see are individuals who construct meaning through a sense of intrinsic relevance and self-typification. I have described the ecumenical lifeworld as an environment that spans individual and organizational system boundaries. Living on the system boundary requires an ability to hold, at times, the dynamic tension of opposing views. Holding this tension is far different from pure relativistic thinking. As Fowler's stages of conjunctive and universalizing faith, and Parks' stage of convictional commitment describe, this marks a transition to wisdom, a maturity that is more inclusive, tolerant, and appreciative of ambiguity, and oriented toward building community. According to Parks, it is a period that opens an engagement with mystery and the ability to see simplicity on the other side of complexity. We acknowledge our interdependence; a self that is both connected yet distinct. We realize the limitations of life, and the dialectical nature of our relationship to it and others revealing the emergence of a deeper self. It is a time that Parks describes as allowing for both needing and giving, weakness and strength, and tenderness and assertiveness. We are able to enlarge others without the anxiety of being diminished ourselves.

These characteristics are typical in the stories of the participants and emerge as some of the dominant images in their lifeworld. These images and the language of repentance, healing and reconciliation among the religious traditions underpin a process of becoming more human. One participant, ordained in the Eastern Rite, shared a notion from his tradition of eastern spirituality stating "to allow yourself to be more human, you are becoming more like God." The ecumenist is called on to be the herald of a future vision of the church, in many ways a prophetic vision. But like the prophet or the reformer, this is a marginal world, where courage and risk-taking are a daily component in the construction of the lifeworld.

The final factor in this model of praxis is perhaps the most important clue, yet maybe the most elusive and challenging to describe and understand; how do individuals sustain themselves in the complexity of boundary roles and embracing difference? For the participants in this study it was a deep and enduring sense of ecumenical spirituality. Ecumenical spirituality is spirituality for the long haul, nurtured by loving patience, a hopeful perseverance, and a dedication to building relationships that cross traditional boundaries. When we approach the topic of ecumenical spirituality we are moving closer to the "locus of meaning" in their lifeworld. This meaning is constructed in relationship not in institutional structures. One ecumenist described ecumenical spirituality as a process of discovery: "we don't build the kingdom of God, we discover the kingdom of God." This discovery is inextricable from a spirituality that continually strives to understand and heal the divisions within the church. It is living in this sense of discovery that moves closer to a process Gros (1993) called a "hermeneutics of piety." This is what the intrinsic or inherent nature of "ecumenical being" is about in this study. In the voices of spirituality echoed in these narratives, it may all be very simple; being ecumenical is what it means to be Christian. The two are inseparable. Ecumenical spirituality serves as a life giving process which holds a complex, exhilarating, frustrating and systemic change in some sense of individual and communal balance.

We know from our discussion of the stages of cognitive and faith development that these individuals show a marked ability to operate at a post-formal, dialectical level. What does this tell us about their sense of spirituality? I believe it sets the foundation for a deep, relational and multi-faceted spirituality that is manifest in different expressions. We see this distinctive quality in the narrative accounts that frame spirituality in terms of ecumenical prayer and worship, learning and teaching, becoming more human, and building lasting relationships.

The open systems term equifinality is an appropriate directional descriptor for this spirituality. Equifinality holds the final state can be reached by any number of sets of initial conditions and by different means (von Bertalanffy,1968). This thinking replaces the causal-linear premise that the final state of a living system is unequivocally determined by the initial conditions. If an individual or group feel they are holding all of the "initial conditions" it is likely that they will use all the power and persuasion they can to be sure there is only one path.

The question now is how we mine this experience of the ecumenical lifeworld, incorporating the lessons from human development, social and organization dynamics and ecumenical spirituality in order to translate a general understanding of sustaining "self" and "others" in the challenging work of dialogue and collective meaning-making. The qualities that seem to standout are faith, discipline, compassion, truthfulness and a striving for wholeness. Several of these qualities are described by Peter Senge in his concept of "personal mastery."

Faith, from the Latin *fides* denotes trust. While the early usage was most often in the context of religious belief, the word *faith* came into Middle English from Old French in the Middle Ages and was associated with loyalty, fealty, and allegiance. Faith expresses a process that is grounded in a fulfilling sense of trust. The Protestant theologian Paul Tillich (1956) described faith as one's "ultimate concern." While by definition this ultimate concern might be anything from worldly preoccupation to the infinite, we find that Tillich saw disappointment for those who look for the ultimate in the mundane. Since faith is a state of being ultimately concerned, it carries with it a total sense of oneself; it is a centered act which is both unconscious and conscious. As reflected in the writing of Soren Kierkegaard (1960) and Gabriel Marcel (1951), faith is an expression of freedom, the most centered act of our will. Faith is not belief. Belief is based on evidence and probability. Faith is not incompatible with doubt because there will always be ultimate risk attached to ultimate concern. Faith is not a form of knowledge with limited evidence supported by external authority

Faith is part of community. Every act of faith depends on an expression of faith. Our way of expression is through language and symbols. The language of faith comes from the community. This raises the question: How does one experience individual spiritual freedom in the face of constraints by the community on the content or practice of individual faith? Tillich described this as the critical balance between the individual and the community. The community that chooses to suppress all freedom and binds its members in legalism and dogmatism, removes the ability of the individual to both risk and express courage in seeking an ultimate concern. In effect it prevents the individual from growing in "adult faith" because the dynamic of dependency is always present, keeping the person sheltered from new insights and awareness. The community in Tillich's mind needs to build into its raison d'être the ability to be self-critical. He referred to this as the "protestant principle."

We shy away from the word discipline in our contemporary culture because it connotes punishment or an unpleasant regime of demands on us physically or mentally. The root word for discipline is disciple, which means pupil. Learning is a relationship, one that requires practice and a continual dialogue between teacher and pupil. When thinking about discipline as a force for our own sustainability we can say that it draws us to focus and be intentional. Discipline in many minds sounds more like compliance but in reality discipline is a cornerstone of commitment. When we commit ourselves we give ourselves to something bigger. The author and poet David Whyte (2001) says; "sooner or later we admit that we cannot do it all, that whatever our contribution, the story is much larger than our own and we are all in the gift of older stories that we are only now joining" (p. 95).

Truthfulness, compassion and wholeness are all qualities Senge describes in "personal mastery." Personal mastery is a set of qualities built around one's ability to continually create, shape and clarify a personal vision. This vision is not simply a "blue sky" imaginary place in the future. It is a very defined and substantive point that requires a realistic and critical assessment of one's current reality. Senge used the term "creative tension" to describe the dynamics between our current reality and vision. This space of creative tension is one filled with possibility. It is an energized field open to new learning, while sharing and challenging mental models. One can feel the creative tension in the lives of these ecumenists in the midst of the unfolding of their own vision into the shared vision of their lifeworld.

The commitment to truth is an ongoing quest. It does not mean settling in on one definitive truth. Senge (1990) states it is our willingness to challenge our dearly held mental models and broaden the perspective of our vision; "The power of truth, seeing reality more and more as it is, cleansing the lens of perception, awakening from self-imposed distortions of reality-different expressions of a common principle in almost all the world's great philosophic and religious systems" (p. 161). In some ways commitment to truth reminds me of an expanding breath inhaling what brings life into our being and exhaling the staleness of our worn out thoughts, attitudes and actions.

Compassion begins with awareness. While we associate it most often with its empathic quality of feelings for another, compassion is also a state of mind and a way of being. Compassion is essential to the values of community. The singular form of this word from Hebrew means womb. What an amazing image of sustaining life in a community being held and nourish as if it were in a womb.

The image of wholeness stands out because in essence that is what we seek, the call to wholeness in ourselves, our communities and the world. It is the ecumenical vision. We must remember wholeness is not sameness and unity not uniformity. Kinnamon (1992) states that *koinonia*: "not only accepts diversity as part of Christian unity, it celebrates it" and "[*koinonia*] implies that our diversity is to be used for the common good" (p. 69/5).

All of these qualities lead us toward authenticity and congruence between what we hold as our deepest values and actions. Argyris and Schon (1974) described this quest for authentic self and behavior in their description of theories-in-action. They spoke of how individuals and organizations frequently have an espoused theory filled with their values and idealized action only to find that their theory-in-use is a far cry from what they espouse.

At a time when globally we grow closer together as a result of information technology and economic interdependence, we remain in most ways a fractured world searching for authenticity. This revisited model of ecumenical praxis built around cognitive development, social construction and spirituality and personal mastery offers some important lessons for all of us who seek to find peaceful, collaborative and creative ways to address the critical issues of our time and the future. Freire (1973) wrote if we are unable to perceive the critical themes of our time we will eventually be carried off in the wake of change. If we are to achieve such a place then we need to benefit from a critical consciousness, participative styles of leadership and action and a systemic understanding of our interdependence as a planetary community. The ecumenical exemplars whose stories enlighten our understanding of embracing the challenges and rewards of differences, for them this model of ecumenical praxis is a window to emancipation and freedom.

REFERENCES

Argyris, C., & Schon, D. (1974). *Theory in practice*. San Francisco: Jossey-Bass.
Argyris, C. (1990). *Overcoming organizational defenses*. Boston: Allyn and Bacon.

Basseches, M. (1984). Dialectical thinking as metasystematic forms of cognitive organization. In M. Commons, et.al. (Eds.) *Beyond formal operations: Late adolescent and adult cognitive development*. New York: Praeger.

Bentz, V. (1989). *Becoming mature: Childhood ghosts and spirits in adult life*. New York: Aldine de Gruyter.

Berger, P.,& Luckmann, T. (1967). *The social construction of reality*. New York: Doubleday.

Berger, P., & Luckmann, T. (1967). *The structures of the lifeworld*. Evanston, IL: Northwestern University Press.

Bohm, D. (1990). *On dialogue*. Ojai, CA.

Bohm, D. (1994). *Thought as a system*. New York: Routledge.

Ellinor, L., & Gerard, G. (1998). *Dialogue; rediscover the transforming power of conversation*. New York: John Wiley.

Fowler, J.W. (1981). *Stages of faith: The psychology of human development and the quest for meaning*. San Francisco: Harper & Row.

Fowler, J. W. (1984). *Becoming adult, becoming Christian*. San Francisco: Harper Collins.

Freire, P. (1970). (Trans. M.R. Ramos). *Pedagogy of the oppressed*. New York: Seabury Press.

Freire, P. (1973). (Trans. M. R. Ramos). *Education for critical consciousness*. New York: Continuum Publishing.

Goleman, D. (1995). *Emotional Intelligence*. New York: Bantam.

Gramsci, A. (1971). (Trans. Q. Hoare & G. N. Smith). *Selections from the prison notebooks of Antonio Gramsci*. New York: International Publishers.

Gros, J. (1993). Towards a hermeneutics of piety for the ecumenical movement. *Ecumenical Trends*, January, Vol. 22(1), 1–12.

Habermas, J. (1971). Trans. J. Shapiro. *Knowledge and human interest*. Boston: Beacon Press.

Habermas, J. (1984). Trans. T. McCarthy. *The theory of communicative action. Volume One: Reason and the rationalization of society*. Boston: Beacon Press.

Habermas, J. (1987). Trans. T. McCarthy. *The theory of communicative action. Volume Two: Lifeworld and system: A critique of functional reason*. Boston: Beacon Press.

Husserl, E. (1970). *The idea of phenomenology*. The Hague: Martinus Nijhoff.

Isaacs, W. (1999). *Dialogue and the art of thinking together*. New York: Currency/Doubleday.

John Paul II. (1995). Encyclical Letter. *Ut Unum Sint*. Boston: St. Paul Media

Kegan, R. (1994). *In over our heads: The mental demands of modern life*. Cambridge: Harvard University Press.

Kelly, J. (1990). Spirals not cycles: Towards an analytic approach to the sources and stages of ecumenism. *Review of Religious Research*, Vol. 32(1), 5–15.

Kierkegaard, S. (1960). (Trans. G. Anderson). P. Rhodes, (Ed.). *Diary of Soren Kierkegaard*. New York: Philosophical Library.

Kinnamon, M. (1992). The nature of the unity we seek. *Ecumenical Trends*, May Vol. 21(5), 3–7.

Kinnamon, M. (1993). Report from the fifth world conference on Faith and Order. *Ecumenical Trends*, Vol. 22(9), 142–145.

Marcel, G. (1951). (Trans. K. Karrer). Being and having. Boston: Beacon Press.

Miles, R. (1980). *Macro organizational behavior*. Glenview, IL: Scott-Foresman.

Parks, S. (1986). *The critical years*. San Francisco: Harper Collins.

Parks, S (2000). *Big questions, worthy dreams*. San Francisco: Jossey-Bass

Schutz, A. (1967). *The phenomenology of the social world*. Evanston, IL: Northwestern University Press.

Schutz, A. (1970). (Wagner, H. Ed.). *Alfred Schutz on phenomenology and social relations*. Chicago: University of Chicago.

Senge, P. (1990). *The fifth discipline*. New York: Doubleday.

Tillich, P. (1956). *Dynamics of faith*. New York: Harper.

von Bertalanffy, L. (1968). *General systems theory*. New York: Brazilier.

Whyte, D. (2001). *Crossing the unknown sea: Work as a pilgrimage of identity*. New York: Riverhead Books.

ABOUT THE CONTRIBUTORS

Marie A. Conn, Professor of Religious Studies, holds a Ph.D. from the University of Notre Dame.

Carolynne Ervin, Coordinator of the Spiritual Direction Practicum, holds an M.A. from Creighton University.

Karen J. Getzen, Assistant Professor of English, holds a Ph.D. from Temple University.

Steven Guerriero, Dean of the School of Graduate Studies, holds a Ph.D. from Fielding Graduate University.

Mary Helen Kashuba, SSJ, Professor of French and Russian, holds a DML from Middlebury College.

Barbara C. Lonnquist, Associate Professor of English, holds a Ph.D. from the University of Pennsylvania.

Thérèse McGuire, SSJ, Professor of Art and Art History (ret.), holds a Ph.D. from New York University.

Carol M. Pate, Associate Professor of Education, holds an Ed.D. from Indiana University.

Nancy Porter, Associate Professor of Psychology, holds a Ph.D. from University of Pennsylvania.

CPSIA information can be obtained at www.ICGtesting.com
Printed in the USA
BVOW020852200412

288139BV00001B/4/P

9 780761 858782